ESSENTIALS
of CRM

Essentials Series

The Essentials Series was created for busy business advisory and corporate professionals. The books in this series were designed so that these busy professionals can quickly acquire knowledge and skills in core business areas.

Each book provides need-to-have fundamentals for those professionals who must:

- Get up to speed quickly, because they have been promoted to a new position or have broadened their responsibility scope.

- Manage a new functional area.

- Brush up on new developments in their area of responsibility.

- Add more value to their company or clients.

Other books in this series include:

Essentials of Accounts Payable,
Mary S. L. Schaeffer

Essentials of Capacity Management,
Reginald Tomas Yu-Lee

Essentials of Corporate Performance Management,
George T. Friedlob, Lydia Schleifer, and Franklin J. Plewa

For more information on any of the above titles, please visit www.wiley.com

ESSENTIALS
of CRM

A Guide to Customer Relationship Management

Bryan Bergeron

WILEY

Library of Congress Cataloging-in-Publication Data

Bergeron, Bryan P.
    Essentials of CRM : a guide to customer relationship management /
    Bryan P. Bergeron.
        p. cm. -- (Essentials series)
    "Published simultaneously in Canada."
    Includes index.
    ISBN 0-471-20603-2 (pbk. : alk. paper)
     1. Customer relations--Management. I. Title. II. Series.

HF5415.5 .B454 2002
658.8'12--dc21   2001008002

10 9 8 7 6 5 4 3 2 1

To Miriam Goodman

Contents

Preface

Every company is involved in customer relationship management (CRM)—even if only in an ad hoc manner—and every CEO should be familiar with the techniques and technologies at his or her disposal. To this end, the goal of this book is to provide the reader with exposure to these techniques and technologies of CRM. Specifically, the *Essentials of CRM* explores examples of customer relationship management that work—and those that don't—with the help of easy-to-understand vignettes. The book assumes an intelligent executive-level reader who may be unaware of the particular vernacular of the customer service field or not know how to recognize a superior CRM formula. The reader will come to appreciate the many uses of CRM, from actively developing a following of profitable customers to turning nonprofitable customers away in cost-saving maneuvers.

Reader Return on Investment

After reading the following chapters you will be able to:

- Understand CRM from historical, economic, technical, and customer perspectives (i.e., the genesis of CRM, how to calculate ROI, the technologies available, and how to evaluate customer satisfaction with the methods chosen for implementation).

- Understand the significance of CRM on the company's bottom line, both long- and short-term.

- Understand how CRM professionals work and think, including why customer service representatives tend to be the lowest paid staff on the corporate payroll.

- Use a set of specific recommendations to establish and manage a CRM effort.

- Understand the technologies, including their tradeoffs, that can be used to implement a CRM service.

- Appreciate best practices—what works, why it works, and how to evaluate a successful CRM effort.

Organization of This Book

This book is organized into modular topics related to CRM. It is divided into the following chapters:

Chapter 1: Overview. The first chapter of this book provides an overview of the key concepts involved in CRM.

Chapter 2: The Customer. This chapter covers CRM from the customer's perspective. Topics include customer expectations, loyalty, touch points, The Loyalty Effect, and customer behavior.

Chapter 3: The Corporation. Taking the perspective of the corporation, this chapter explores the internal jobs, processes, and technology issues faced by businesses involved in a CRM effort. Topics include crafting a comprehensive view of the customer, employee incentives, corporate culture, rewarding employee performance, and strategic partnerships and alliances.

Chapter 4: Technology. This chapter explores the many technologies available for CRM and how the appropriate technology can be used to leverage human resources in a company. Topics include customer profiling, data warehousing, pervasive computing, and security systems.

Chapter 5: eCRM. With the advent of the Web, CRM has taken on a new meaning. As described in this chapter, the ease with which large volumes of data can be captured from online transactions and the technologies available to analyze this data are changing the face of CRM. Topics include the Web and E-commerce, customer tracking, customer support surrogates, and real-time CRM.

Chapter 6: Evaluating Solutions. This chapter explores how the various approaches to CRM can be evaluated. Topics range from the effectiveness of the various technologies available for CRM to the effect of specific CRM processes on price, customer expectations, and customer service.

Chapter 7: Economics of CRM. Exploring the possibilities of CRM costs money. This chapter looks at the financial outlay for various approaches to CRM, as well as the expected ROI that can reasonably be expected from each approach. Topics include Web initiatives, technology-assisted CRM, ROI, and economic timelines.

Chapter 8: Getting There. The final chapter provides some concrete examples of the resources, time, and costs involved in embarking on a practical CRM effort. Topics range from the implementation challenges, the economy, and risk management to working with vendors.

Further Reading. This appendix lists some of the more relevant works in the area of CRM, at a level appropriate to a CEO or upper-level CRM manager.

How to Use This Book

For those new to CRM, the best way to tackle the subject is to simply read through each chapter sequentially; however, because each chapter is written as a stand-alone module, readers interested in, for example, Web-based CRM strategies, can go directly to Chapter 5, "eCRM."

Throughout the book, "In the Real World" sections provide real-world examples of how CRM is being used to improve the bottom line and provide insight into customer behavior. Similarly, a "Tips

& Techniques" section in each chapter offers concrete steps that the reader can take to benefit from a CRM initiative. Key terms are highlighted and defined throughout the book, as well as available in the Glossary at the end of the book. In addition, readers who want to delve deeper into the business, technical, or cultural aspects of CRM are encouraged to consult the list of books and publications listed in the Further Reading section.

Acknowledgments

Creating a book on relationships is a team effort that requires the focused cooperation of a variety of experts, each with their own focus and areas of contribution. In this regard, I would like to thank my enduring editorial associate, Miriam Goodman, an accomplished artist in traditional as well as digital media, and a poet, teacher, photographer, and author. Among other things, Miriam was responsible for adding a spark of life to the flesh of this book.

To my readers, reviewers, and researchers; Rosalind Bergeron, my sister, business partner, and attorney in Silicon Valley; and Ron Rouse, Software System Specialist in Educational Computing at Harvard Medical School, for their time, inspiration, and constructive criticism. Finally, special thanks to my editor at John Wiley & Sons, Sheck Cho, for his insight and encouragement.

CHAPTER 1

Overview

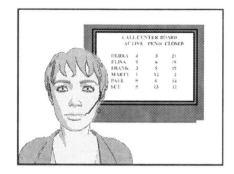

In today's economy, companies want a loyal following and quality customers. They also want their image in the marketplace to be positive, despite the need to contain expenses on unprofitable customers. Paradoxically, even though the United States is evolving into a service economy, customer service satisfaction is at an all-time low. As explained in more detail in Chapters 2 and 3, this perception may be partially the result of measures a CEO puts in place to save costs, which make a bad impression and tax the patience of the customer, and partly the result of rising customer expectations.

For example, there may be a corporate initiative to contain costs by rationing customer support services, but the customer may not be informed about this change or told what to expect. Similarly, customer relationship management (CRM) initiatives that fail to incorporate appropriate technologies often perform below expectations. Such technologies can help service reps provide customers with directed assistance in a cost-effective manner. Today's customers expect more after their early dotCom experience, where everything was either free or heavily subsidized.

CRM is fundamentally about the ongoing relationship between people—the suppliers and customers of goods and services. In this

The Stats on CRM

CRM was born around 1997 as a means of redefining the customer-company relationship through computer-based tools. In theory, every customer-company interaction can be recorded, allowing a company to proactively provide the best customer service possible while creating a database of customer preferences that can be reviewed by sales, marketing, and management. The data can then be used to reduce costs and improve employee productivity.

In reality, CRM doesn't come cheap, in terms of either time or expense. A typical CRM installation costs approximately $500,000 for a midsize company and $3 million or more for a large company. In addition, about 80 percent of CRM sales goes to large corporations, primarily because that's where the money is.

Few CRM vendors deal with small companies, in part because the work to implement a CRM solution for a small company is virtually the same as that for a midsize company; however, most small companies can't afford the six-figure price tag. CRM may be young, but it's serious business. Sales of CRM software and services were about $25 billion in 2001 and are expected to grow to well over double that by 2005.

context, a customer is someone who has paid for a service or product. That is, they have already gone through the sales process and are using their purchase. The closure of the sales process consummates the customer-company relationship. In other words, CRM isn't about directly attracting new customers. This isn't to say that good CRM doesn't attract new customers—it generally does—but existing customers, not new ones, are the primary population served.

The management component of CRM implies a skilled use of resources, as opposed to a haphazard, reactionary attempt to put out

> **KEY TERM**
>
> **Customer relationship management (CRM)** The dynamic process of managing a customer-company relationship such that customers elect to continue mutually beneficial commercial exchanges and are dissuaded from participating in exchanges that are unprofitable to the company.

fires. CRM is a process. Like a standardized manufacturing process or computer algorithm, CRM is a technology that specifies the steps needed to consistently achieve a particular result. Following a process greatly increases the odds of consistent, repeatable, measurable results. Using an assembly-line approach to manufacturing a widget, for example, should provide widgets of known quality and cost, with a known resource investment and outcome.

CRM is concerned with the dynamics of an existing customer-company relationship. The process of CRM is dynamic in that working assumptions and the appropriate actions may change, based on fluctuations in the environment or in the customer-company relationship. This implies that CRM involves continual attention to the customer-company relationship, in terms of time, money, or other resources.

CRM is not part of the sales process and shouldn't be confused with sales relationship management (SRM), which often assumes that every prospect should buy from the company. Salespeople are rewarded for sales, not for the long-term cost to their company. If a customer turns out to be a drain on the company, it's not the sales department's problem, but it becomes a customer service problem.

Dissecting the definition further, notice that the customer is ultimately in control of the relationship. The customer can elect to continue the relationship or walk away. In this regard, the definition also implies that the company is doing most of the work of maintaining a mutually beneficial relationship. In this situation, the customer may contribute only a modicum of effort in maintaining the relationship, such as taking the time to order a widget from the company instead of placing the order with a competitor.

The asymmetry of the relationship differentiates CRM from partnership relationship management (PRM). In PRM, the relationship is generally between equal partners, as defined by a written contractual agreement. Although any party may elect to walk away, there may be monetary or other mutually agreed-on penalties for doing that. In contrast, the asymmetry of the customer-company relationship is usually established by law. Customers have certain rights, such as their ability to return merchandise in exchange for their money, as defined by state and federal law.

The stipulation of a mutually beneficial commercial exchange is the underlying incentive for CRM. Unless there is a reasonable return on what can be a sizable CRM investment, there is no motivation to devote time and energy to CRM. CRM seeks a balance between attracting the largest number of profitable customers that fit within the mission of the company (assuming the company is going for market share) or a smaller number of profitable customers (when the goal is to maximize profits). Dell Computer, Chevrolet, and Dockers take the former approach, whereas Apple Computer, Porsche, and Armani take the latter.

CRM is one way to keep customers that would otherwise go elsewhere. As such, CRM is a way to manage a company's resources in a way that maximizes long-term return on investment (ROI), although this doesn't necessarily mean retaining old customers. The goal is not simply to please customers—that's easy enough to do by giving product away with free, at-home, lifetime service. Rather, the goal is to foster the right kind of repeat customers.

Note that the commercial exchange is decoupled from the relationship. That is, the customer-company relationship remains even if no future commercial exchanges occur. The relationship may continue nonetheless, as when a customer calls the company for product support, to exchange a defective item, or simply to complain about the product or service. A customer may also call or write about their total satisfaction with the company's service. In the context of CRM, however, most customer contact with the company is assumed to be problem-oriented, and the resolution of the problem usually comes at a cost to the company. In some cases, this cost represents an investment in the future of the company, as when customers find problems and bugs for the company to fix, which can result in better products. Many companies involved in software development use this approach of intentionally releasing a product too early in the release cycle, using paying customers as beta test subjects.

The dynamics of the customer-company relationship usually change when the relationship becomes unprofitable to the company. In this situation, even though the customer can decide when to walk away from the relationship, the company's investment in maintaining the relationship may be minimal and may be overshadowed by the work invested by the customer. For example, a customer may stay on hold for a half hour, simply to be told by a customer service representative that the company can do nothing to help rectify the problem.

The company can actively dissuade customers from participating in exchanges (e.g., telephone calls to the customer support department) that are unprofitable. Placing customers on indefinite hold, ignoring letters from customers complaining of poor service, and treating customers with a negative attitude or even rudeness are means used to dissuade customer contact with the company. When customer expectations are managed, these dissuaders can be less painful.

Unprofitable customers aren't limited to those that cost the company money in the short term but also include customers who have limited probability of engaging in profitable exchanges in the future. Consider a charge card customer who either doesn't use his card or uses it for only a few dollars worth of purchases a month and pays his balance in full. In the short term, he costs the company money every month because of the expense of mailing the statement and handling his payment. Whether he will be a profitable customer in the future or an unprofitable or revenue neutral customer is a judgment call that should be made based on information the charge card company has about the customer's identity and past buying patterns.

With no other information, the company might be inclined to dissuade the customer from engaging in future business—by raising his interest rate, for example; however, if the company learns that the customer is about to graduate from law school, it's probably in the company's best interest to keep the customer happy. Conversely, if the company learns that the spendthrift is unemployed, in the middle of a divorce, and has a high likelihood of filing for bankruptcy in the near future, it shouldn't go out of its way to please the customer.

Three Roommates

In order to illustrate the complexity of the issues that CRM is intended to address, consider the following vignette.

In a spacious, three-bedroom apartment in a university town, three 20-something roommates, Debra, Jen, and Paul, are sitting at the kitchen table, discussing their upcoming house party. Paul, a graduate student in history, and Debra, an attractive undergraduate art major, are both single; however, unlike Paul, Debra seems to have a never-ending supply of prospects (i.e., dates). Jen, a waitress at a nearby restaurant, is in a serious relationship with the restaurant's manager, Bob, and often disappears from the apartment on weekends when he drives them to the beach.

As the three look over the party notice and discuss how many invitations each should hand out to friends and acquaintances, it becomes obvious that each has different expectations regarding the party. Paul is looking forward to the party as a means of meeting potential prospects. Debra is simply looking to have a good time; if someone happens to catch her eye, all the better. Jen, in contrast, wants to show off her boyfriend.

When the night of the party arrives, the weather cooperates and the turnout is better than expected. Perhaps one hundred men and women, with occupations from students to office managers, are enjoying the music, food, and conversation. During the party, Paul manages to dance with a half-dozen women and secures a phone number from three of them. Debra, as usual, is constantly surrounded by men vying for her attention. She gives her phone number to four of them that she considers the most handsome, intelligent men at the party and distances herself—politely—from the other suitors. Jen, in contrast, is focused on Bob, showing him off to her friends, dancing with only him, and enjoying the festive atmosphere. Bob seems to be genuinely enjoying himself and captivated by Jen; only once did Jen notice his eyes stray to Debra and linger there for a few moments.

On the following morning, during a major cleanup operation, the three roommates agree that the party was generally a success. Paul has three prospects to call and hopefully get to know better over the next few weeks. Likewise, Debra expects calls from the few men that seemed the most promising. Jen, the least enthusiastic of the three, is a little jealous of Debra and wonders about Bob's commitment to their relationship.

Key Concepts

The story of Debra, Jen, and Paul, to be continued throughout this book, illustrates several key concepts regarding CRM.

What CRM Isn't

The story highlights the difference between customer, sales, and partnership relationship management. Debra, Jen, and Paul are in a mutually beneficial business relationship, in that they share space, contribute equally to the rent, and presumably share the responsibility for keeping the common areas clean and orderly. In this example, the three room-

TIPS & TECHNIQUES

Understanding the Value of CRM

Before embarking on a CRM initiative, senior management should have a good idea of the potential value of CRM to the organization. In other words, what's wrong with the current way of conducting business, from a customer relations perspective? The three key questions to ask are:

- How much money could be saved with a viable CRM system in place? That is, what are the potential cost reductions in sales, marketing, and customer service?

- How much could a CRM system increase revenues, in terms of increased sales volume, greater size and frequency of orders, and, ultimately, more profit per customer?

- How much will it cost to implement a CRM system, keeping in mind that most companies spend at least as much on employee training as they do on CRM software.

CRM is often touted as a means of improving customer satisfaction, which in turn improves long-term customer loyalty. It's also ostensibly part of a public relations campaign to increase the company's image. Finally, many CRM companies claim that their products make it easier for employees to do their jobs; however, these subjective metrics are difficult, if not impossible, to measure quantitatively.

mates take joint responsibility for managing their relationship. They share equal responsibility for their partner relationship management. Similarly, Paul is single, not in a relationship, and in the market for prospects. His interest in the party was to identify and qualify potential women to date. In establishing a rapport with a few of the women at the party, he identified several women he plans to call later and potentially see again. Similarly, even though Debra has several ongoing relationships, she is always on the lookout for better prospects. The commodity they each have to sell is themselves. Both Paul and Debra are involved in sales relationship management.

In addition, Debra is involved in several ongoing, but apparently not very serious, relationships, and she knows when to drop a guy so that she can concentrate on the better prospects. In this regard, Debra represents a company involved in an ad hoc CRM initiative, and her current relationships represent customers. She knows how and when to give a suitor encouragement, and when to give him the cold shoulder.

Importance of Self-Knowledge

In the story, the three roommates apparently know themselves, at least as far as relationships go. They are aware of their needs, what they're willing to give up and contribute to a relationship or relationships, and what kind of partner is most suitable for them.

As an analogy for CRM, the three roommates' story highlights the importance of corporate culture in a customer-company relationship. Although customer-focused approaches to business are now in vogue, there's a danger in not looking inward from time to time. The corporate culture, including employee satisfaction, ultimately affects how customers are perceived and treated. Although there's no right or wrong culture, the issue is internal consistency. If the customer support staff is told to help customers in every way possible, but the customer support department is severely understaffed and kept out of the loop when new product features are introduced, not only will the company-customer relationship suffer, but the company will waste internal resources as well.

Role of Technology

Even though most of the issues surrounding CRM are interpersonal, technology can help. In the story, Paul plans to use the telephone to continue his dialogue with the three women he met at the house party and perhaps arrange future dates. Similarly, Bob and Jen rely on transportation technology for their weekend getaways.

There's a Process

Paul, Debra, and Jen go about their socializing according to generally accepted etiquette. Although it may seem completely random and by chance, relationships usually develop according to established social norms or processes. Consider how most relationships form: Someone notices someone else, either because they share an experience or pastime or they are physically attracted, or perhaps because of a chance encounter (e.g., reaching for the same container of soap in a grocery store or meeting at a house party).

Whatever the nature of the initial contact, whether the meeting becomes anything more depends on one or both parties making an effort to connect with the other person. The driving force may be that one party controls something the other wants, or because an attraction exists, or simply because no other choices are available. Once a relationship is established, there is a generally recognized process for maintaining it. In Jen's case, it means inviting her boyfriend to the party, showing him off a bit to her friends, and doing her best to see that he has a good time. Similarly, Bob reciprocates, calling Jen and including her in his activities.

Finite Longevity of the Relationship

There is always a question of the longevity of a relationship. Even though Jen is apparently dedicated to keeping their relationship alive, she couldn't help notice Bob's wandering eyes. Assuming they get along, if Bob and Jen were stranded together on a deserted island, there would be no issue of outside threats to their relationship, until they were rescued. Unless there is a long-term need that each fulfills in the other, their relationship will eventually fail.

A lasting relationship usually requires some give and take from all parties involved in the relationship. In a relationship between two people, if one person changes unilaterally to meet the other's needs at the expense of his or her own, eventually, he or she will become resentful and the relationship will be threatened. In Jen's case, this threat might take the form of another relationship or, if things progress to marriage, end in divorce.

When the relationship involves a customer and a company, the customer can't reasonably expect to have free, unlimited customer support for life. To proactively limit their exposure to customers who would misuse customer support, many companies limit the customer-company relationship by instituting limits on free customer support. Customers who elect to pay for continued support, either by the hour or on a subscription basis, determine the extent and length of the relationship. That is, they contribute to the relationship.

Need for Consistency

A critical aspect of any customer-company relationship is the need for the company to present a consistent image. Paul, Jen, and Debra don't change into someone else when their guests arrive, or in front of their dates. Similarly, Disney protects the illusion that its characters are real by prohibiting them from being out in public unless they are fully costumed.

A single inconsistency in behavior can irrevocably change the perception of a person or character. For example, when Darth Vader is unmasked in *Return of the Jedi,* revealing an avuncular old man, the revelation softens his image forever, even in reruns of the earlier Star Wars movies.

The same can be said for the image developed by a corporation. For example, a "green" corporation found dumping toxic waste down the public drainage system can't expect to recover its initial public image. Companies, like people, are judged more on their behavior than on their words.

Need to Manage Expectations

Perhaps the greatest challenge in managing an ongoing relationship is establishing and managing joint expectations. For example, is loyalty assumed? From both parties? What about trust? What are the ground rules? Is the current exchange a one-time event or the start of a life-long relationship?

Debra's expectations regarding loyalty are apparently different from Jen's expectations surrounding her relationship with Bob; however, it's unclear how the expectations of Jen's boyfriend and Debra's suitors differ. In managing customer-company relationships, both the customer and the company need to know when to walk away from the relationship and when to keep trying, based on short- and long-term expectations.

Role of Context

The context at the start of a relationship affects both short- and long-term expectations. If Paul had introduced himself as Debra's boyfriend, the women he danced with would likely have had different expectations of his requests to dance. That is, presumably his requests would have been perceived as part of being a proper host and not as any sort of advance for a potential relationship.

Similarly, a customer at a booth at a ballgame shouldn't expect a special break on prices because the booth operator—who may be a temporary hire—knows that he'll likely never see the customer again. In other words, in the context of their current business transaction, there's no future in the relationship and no reason to make concessions to a particular customer.

Relationships are Complex

Life—and relationships—is complex, even for three people sharing an apartment. Unspoken internal rules (e.g., Jen's boyfriend is off-limits to Debra) as well as external rules must be followed. For example, the rent has to be paid on time. There are also rules of privacy and security. Debra's room may be off-limits to her roommates. Her roommates expect Debra to respect their privacy. The three roommates have the luxury of frequent encounters so that their concerns can be aired and resolved— a luxury that most customer-company relationships don't have.

In the customer-company relationship, customers can reasonably expect their transactions to be secure and private as well—an expectation that isn't always met. There are external constraints, such as federal and state laws pertaining to a customer's right to privacy; local, regional, and statewide politics; and a variety of social issues to deal with as well. When competitors are added to the mix, the dynamics and assumptions of the system can rapidly become even more complex.

Summary

Customer relationship management (CRM) is fundamentally about managing the relationships among people within an organization and between customers and the company's customer service representatives in order to improve the bottom line. CRM recognizes the role of technology, the importance of self-knowledge, the finite nature of customer-company relationships, and the need for consistency in quality of service. Effective CRM is also based on a process, as opposed to an ad hoc approach, which includes managing customer expectations.

The fragrance always remains in the hand that gives the rose.

Heda Bejar

CHAPTER 2

The Customer

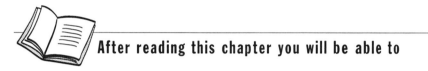

After reading this chapter you will be able to

- Appreciate customer relationship management from the customer's perspective
- Understand the importance of customer expectations in the customer-company relationship
- Understand the significance of brand identity in the customer-company relationship
- Define the Loyalty Effect and how it can be used as a tool to predict and modify customer behavior
- Appreciate the significance of touch points

The focus of most CRM activity is the customer. The company gathers information about the customer, makes a predictive model of customer behavior, and seeks to control customer interactions with the company. The company also manages customer expectations. Because the customer-company relationship can be a lifetime proposition, it makes sense to understand the relationship from the customer's perspective. To help illustrate this perspective, let's continue with the three roommates introduced in Chapter 1.

A Bike for Paul

It's about one month after the house party where Paul met several potential prospects. He has a second date with one of the women, Julie, an avid cyclist who invited Paul to join her on a 30-mile ride. Paul is using the upcoming ride as a good reason to upgrade his existing bike —a clunker that he bought more than eight years ago.

Paul stops by the local bike shop where he's had minor repairs done on his bike over the past four years. The owner, Hank, is friendly, personable, and greets Paul by name when he walks in. In the shop, Paul is inundated by choices of frames, components, helmets, bike locks, water bottles, and other accessories. Hank takes Paul aside and shows him several brand-name mountain bikes that would suit him and fit within his price range. Hank also shows Paul a no-name bike that is almost half the price of the cheapest brand-name bike. The frame is not as sturdy, the components aren't as light, and the paint finish isn't as glossy, and the frame has a five-year warranty, but the price is right. In comparison, the brand-name bikes have lifetime warranties on the frames and have much lighter components. Paul takes a handful of brochures home. With the price list in hand, he looks for a better deal on a brand-name bike on the Web.

On the Web, Paul manages to locate one of the brand-name bikes that he liked in Hank's shop—for about $100 less; however, he's uncomfortable about making a major purchase on the Web with a company he hasn't dealt with before. Uncertain of what to do, he calls Hank and asks why he should consider buying the bike from him. Hank emphasizes that he has been in business for 20 years, that he's a certified dealer for the top brands, and that he offers an unconditional one-year shop warranty on all parts and labor that's included in the price of the bike. After a night of deliberations and examining his bank account balance, Paul decides to buy the brand-name bike from Hank. Hank promises to have the bike ready in time for Paul to practice using it before his outing with Julie on Saturday.

When it comes time for Paul to hit the trails with Julie, he is outfitted with a smart-looking bike that allows him to think of the trail—and his date—without worrying that his old tires might go flat or that his brakes might fail on a hill; however, as Paul discovers, even mountain bikes aren't indestructible, and he manages to break two spokes on his rear wheel while navigating through a field of grapefruit-sized rocks. The damage isn't bad enough for him to have to curtail the 30-mile off-road adventure, but there is a noticeable wobble in the wheel, and it will have to be repaired before another outing.

With his and Julie's bikes secured to the rooftop of his car, and on his way to Julie's place for dinner, Paul calls the bike shop just before closing to ask when he can drop his bike off to be repaired. Hank tells him not to worry about it, that he'll come by to pick up the bike on his way to the shop just before noon on Sunday, and that he'll have the bike back to him by Monday evening. As promised, Hank shows up with his van just before noon on Sunday and picks up Paul's bike. He also leaves a loaner bike so that Paul can bike that afternoon if he wants to.

Meanwhile, Julie stopped by to visit Paul and to show him the catalog from a mail-order and Web-based company that she uses to buy her bike accessories. Because she's a member of the company—a privilege she pays $20 a year for—she gets notified of specials, has a free second-day shipping upgrade, and the technical support people are at her disposal. They look through the catalog and locate a set of panniers for Paul's bike so that he can carry a jacket and some extra food on his bike outings. Because Paul is leery about using his charge card to order something on the Web, Julie offers to let Paul add the panniers to her next order so that he can receive the free shipping upgrade and the membership discount.

On Monday, on his way home from the bike shop, Hank drops off Paul's bike—at no charge—and retrieves the loaner bike. Paul is so pleased with the service that he stops by the bike shop on the following Friday to pick up a set of panniers like the ones he had planned to order through a mail-order catalog.

Issues

Paul's encounter with the bike shop owner and Julie's relationship with the mail-order company illustrate several key CRM issues from the customer's perspective:

- A business can manage the customer's expectations regarding the nature and value of the future relationship with the business. The bike shop owner told Paul what to expect of his future relationship with the business: that the shop will fix anything for free for the first year Paul owns the bike. Thus Paul understands that the shop values his business and expects good service in the future.

- Brand identity is often significant in establishing customer expectations. Paul is initially torn between saving money on a no-name bike and the peace of mind and image buying a brand-name bike would bring.

- The integration, accessibility, and consistency of a company's touch points are critical to establishing and maintaining a customer-company relationship. Hank is consistent in his communications to Paul, reassuring Paul that their good relationship will extend into the future.

- Relationship dynamics in a customer-company relationship are complex and based on both known and unknown variables. Both Paul and Hank have to make several assumptions about the future behavior of the other.

- Customer behavior can be predicted by modeling the customer's perception of the customer-company relationship. Paul is averse to giving his personal information out over the Web to an unknown online bike shop and therefore avoids ordering online despite the cost savings.

These issues are explored in the following section.

Managing Customer Expectations

Customers reasonably come to expect certain things—such as a quality product, timely service, and value for their money—from a business relationship. Paul expects his local bike shop to offer personal service and the shops on the Web to offer a larger selection and better prices. His expectations are based largely on personal experience, as well as accounts of experiences from his friends. For example, Julie introduced Paul to a mail-order company that provides good service, in part because she pays an added premium that distinguishes her from other customers.

Rising Customer Expectations

Since the advent of the Web, Paul, like most Internet-savvy consumers, expects more value for his money. Reasonably or not, he expects retail outlets in general to be more responsive and the bike shop in particular to provide better service. He expects Hank to make it worth his while to travel to the bike shop instead of simply picking up the phone or sending an E-mail to place an order. Paul expects to be treated well by Hank, especially because he is considering buying a rather pricey brand-name mountain bike. Similarly, because of his experience with online companies such as Amazon.com, he also expects whatever he orders online to appear on his doorstep by next-day express delivery.

TIPS & TECHNIQUES

Managing Customer Expectations

Although customer expectations are increasing, it's a relative phenomenon. Certainly, customer frustration with infinite loop voice mail support systems is on the rise; however, whether the frustration is caused by rising expectations or simply the futility of repeatedly punching buttons on a phone in order to talk to a real person is debatable. Also, customers who are being well served don't make as much noise as customers who feel slighted.

In order to evaluate the potential value of using a CRM system to better satisfy the support needs of good (profitable) customers, the key questions to ask include:

- What is the competition doing to manage customer expectations? The nearest competition as well as the industry as a whole influences customer expectations.

- How do customer touch points, including phone, fax, E-mail, Web, and in-person, differ from the customer's perspective?

- Other than profitability, what metrics differentiate good and bad customers? Is it the amount of customer support they require, number of transactions per month or year, or average transaction size?

- What touch points tend to be frequented by good customers? What about bad (unprofitable) customers?

For example, suppose it's known that providing more E-mail support meets or exceeds the expectations of proportionately more profitable customers than unprofitable ones. Shifting customer service representatives from, say, phone to E-mail support should improve the bottom line. Determining which customers are good and which ones are bad in a timely fashion is what CRM is all about.

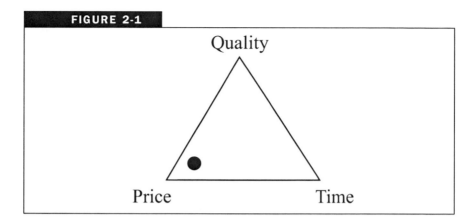

FIGURE 2-1

Quality

Price   Time

Paul has come to expect more—better quality, a better price, and faster service: however, as illustrated in Figure 2-1, companies typically compete in the marketplace on the basis of quality, price, or speed of service. The most successful companies compete on only one of these criteria; few companies can sustain competing in two areas and remain economically viable. For example, the online bike shops compete on the basis of price, whereas the local bike shop competes on quality of service. The local shop can't be expected to match the online bike dealer's price and provide the same high level of service—and stay in business.

One of Hank's challenges is establishing Paul's expectations for the quality of service that he offers. In this regard, Hank is successful in creating what he hopes to be a long-term relationship with Paul from the start of his interactions. First, he puts Paul at ease. He suggests bikes and brands, but he doesn't tell Paul which bike to buy. He is personable, attentive, and responsive to Paul's questions. Furthermore, Hank presents a single personality, and one that's consistent with Paul's previous encounters with Hank. He is also respectful of Paul's time and is truthful, unambiguous, and anticipates Paul's concerns.

Given the quality and level of the initial interaction, Paul reasonably assumes that Hank's commitment to an ongoing relationship is high, and Paul is reassured that Hank's bike shop will be there in the future in the event that he has any problems with his bike. As detailed in the story, Paul's expectations are not only met, they are exceeded.

Privacy and Security Concerns

One reason that Paul doesn't elect to do business with an online bike shop was his concerns regarding the security of his online transactions with an unknown vendor. He doesn't want his charge card information floating freely around the Internet where it can be intercepted and abused.

In reality, security risks aren't limited to Web-based transactions. All charge card activity, whether made in person or in a walk-in retail shop, is transmitted electronically across a network of some type to a central data processing facility; however, the security risks of electronic transactions are usually borne by the charge card company. Most companies limit exposure to $50 or less, as long as a missing card is reported as soon as it's discovered missing or stolen.

The charge card companies use customer databases to verify that charges are within allowable limits and that the current purchase matches past buying behavior. The former check is to make certain that a charge cardholder stays within the agreed-upon credit limit, while the latter determination is intended to flag possibly fraudulent behavior.

For example, if Paul decides to impress Julie by buying her an expensive bracelet, when his charge card is swiped by the jewelry store manager, the transaction may be flagged by the charge card company. It may be flagged because a charge of several hundred dollars for jewelry stands out against a normal buying pattern of $20 to $50 purchases at the campus bookstore. If the charge is flagged, the charge company will deny the charge unless the manager verifies Paul's identity by checking his driver's license. If Paul visits the store in a month to pick up another piece of jewelry in the same price range, the charge card company will most likely not flag the transaction as something out of the ordinary.

Usually, the greatest personal risk with electronic transactions of any kind is related to privacy. In the case of the charge at the jewelry store, Paul's transaction is recorded by the jewelry store as well as the charge card company. The store will likely add Paul's name to their mailing list, possibly inundating him with flyers and specials on engagement rings. If the store is part of a chain that has an online presence, Paul may receive occasional E-mails on specials as well.

The real issue is what the charge card company does with the transaction data. Because the company has access to Paul's demographic information—his age, occupation, mailing address, annual income, spending history, and credit risk—it can sell Paul's address to a variety of vendors. Within weeks of Paul's purchase of his new bike, for example, he could receive subscription offers from bicycle magazines, mail-order catalogs of bicycle accessories, catalogs of outdoors and fitness activity apparel, and offers from travel agencies offering exotic bicycle adventures.

Online retailers are often a significant privacy risk because of the ease and frequency with which they trade and sell customer lists. In many cases, more profit can be made from selling mailing and E-mail lists than in a dotCom's retail product or service. From the customer's perspective, the online retailers with the best privacy policies provide the following features:

- *Warn customers before they interact with the site.* Customers have an opportunity to leave a site before their activity is tracked. This option is akin to the warning given to callers to customer support, where a voice announcement stating that "your conversation may be recorded for training purposes" is made before the customer is connected with a customer service representative.

- *Give customers control over how their information is used.* Customers can accept or reject forwarding of their E-mail, phone, or mailing address information to other vendors.

- *Allow customers to correct inaccurate information.* This is a win-win situation for companies and customers, because customers may want information sent to the right address, and companies don't want to waste money sending flyers and catalogs to the wrong address.

- *Allow customers to see what is being tracked.* This feature can be used to help customers customize their interaction with an online retailer. For example, Amazon.com, which targets customers who want personalized online service, shows customers their latest purchases and searches so they don't have to repeat searches.

- *Allow customers to opt out of any interaction.* Customers don't appreciate being forced into an interaction, such as having to supply their E-mail address in order to view a company's online catalog.

For example, if Paul had decided to purchase a bike online, he would expect that his charge card information would not be released to other companies. He would also expect to be able to remove his E-mail and mailing address from any bulk mailing list. The real issue, however, is that of verification and enforcement. Most online customers believe there is really no way for them to verify that their identity and purchasing profile have not been sold to a company. Companies are constantly changing their online policies (e.g., AOL recently changed its privacy policy to allow it to sell customer information) and because online companies are often acquired, customer information is constantly changing hands.

Brand Identity

Paul's decision to go with a brand-name bicycle was based partly on Hank's recommendations and partly on his perception of the long-term effects (including support) the decision will have on his enjoyment of the bike. The factors Paul considers in deciding to buy a brand-name bike include its higher resale value, the "image" of riding a brand-name bicycle, and the risks of having warranty repairs covered by a no-name bike company.

Paul's decision illustrates how customers don't simply think of a brand as a group of features and functional benefits. After all, a no-name bike might last just as long as a nationally known brand of bike. The best brands are linked to emotional, cultural, and even spiritual qualities, not cold functional qualities. For example, in the bicycle market, Schwinn represented the best that money could buy in the 1950s and 1960s, in part because it represented the "dream machine;" however, despite its success with the 10-speed bike market in the 1970s, Schwinn ignored the mountain bike market of the 1980s as a passing fad. Its bike quickly became "uncool," compared to those produced by Specialized, Trek, Marin, Cannondale, and others that chose to enter the mountain bike market. Today, Schwinn is in the mountain bike market but has to fight for the brand position of "dream machine" with entrenched competition.

Similarly, other successful brands are associated with emotional, not logical or functional, attributes. The Disney brand is known for family fun and entertainment, McDonald's for fun and food, and Nike for performance. The customers' image of these brands is independent of how they, as customers, interact with the company. That is, Nike represents performance regardless of whether the brand appears in a magazine ad, on a TV commercial, in a retail shoe outlet, or on a track star's feet.

Customers think of a brand as encompassing all possible points of contact or touch points (see the following section), and their expectations are identical no matter how they interact with a company. For example, if Hank closes his bike shop, Paul reasonably expects his bike's lifetime frame warranty to be honored at any authorized dealer carrying his brand of bike. Hank certainly adds a personal touch to customer

Nortel Networks

Nortel Networks has the distinction of driving the world's largest CRM implementation initiative. Nortel's challenge is formidable, with 19 legacy systems, more than 50 customer contact centers, and 20,000 call center operators who handle more than 900 toll-free sales and support numbers, 54 million call minutes per month, and 73 million E-mail messages per month. Their goal is to move the company to a single CRM solution that will present a single, global customer view.

support, but Paul expects a certain minimum of support, regardless of the dealer, by virtue of the company behind the brand.

Touch Points

In deciding whether to buy a bike from the local bike shop or shop online, Paul had an opportunity to interact with several touch points—the point of contact between a customer and a company—for each business. When dealing with the online store, the touch points consisted of E-mail for communications and data from the company's Web site. Paul never had an opportunity to talk with anyone on the phone. As such, it wasn't clear to Paul if the physical presence of the online "shop" consisted of a PC in someone's dorm room or a large server in a bicycle manufacturing plant in Taiwan. In contrast, Paul was able to deal with Hank in person, over the phone, fax, mail, and E-mail.

As illustrated in Figure 2-2, customers interact with businesses through multiple touch points. Sometimes only one or two touch points are actually supported, and in other cases there are more potential touch points than customers can or want to access. The most common touch points for a business include:

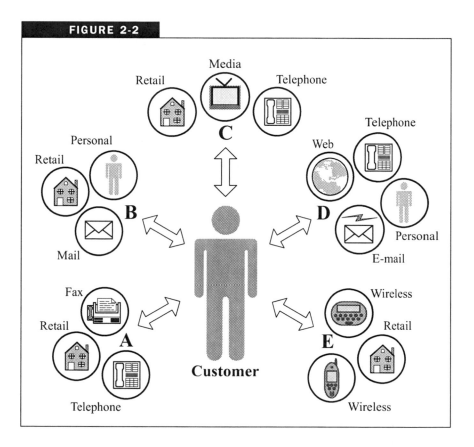

FIGURE 2-2

- *Email.* Responses to E-mail queries, either from customer service representatives or intelligent messaging systems, and notices and advertisements

- *Fax.* Includes proactive faxes that notify customers of specific specials related to their past purchases

- *Mail.* Traditional mail, including flyers and even bills

- *Media.* Advertisements on TV, radio, newspapers, and flyers

- *Personal Contact.* Face-to-face contact in retail outlets

- *Retail Outlet.* The physical storefront

- *Telephone.* Direct phone conversations with customer service representatives, voice messaging, and interaction with systems through push-button menus that use voice synthesis (and voice recognition) to automate common transactions in a simulation of a person-to-person conversation

- *Web.* Lists of frequently asked questions, active searches of databases that may contain product and pricing information, warranty information, and product support areas (The Web is no more and no less important than any other touch point.)

- *Wireless.* Location-independent versions of E-mail, phone, fax, and Web access

In Paul's dealings with Hank, he was pleased to discover that the store's message was consistent through all touch points. That is, Hank didn't try a bait-and-switch sale, using the newspaper to bring Paul into the showroom, only to have none of the advertised bikes in stock. More important, when Paul called to report the broken spokes, Hank not only fulfilled his promise of giving Paul a loaner bike while he made the free repairs, but he went one step farther by picking up the bike and dropping off the loaner as well. In other words, he not only met Paul's expectations, but exceeded them.

Every touch point is critical in providing service and potentially increasing customer satisfaction. In this regard, E-mail, the Web, fax, telephone, personal contact, and even the messages that accompany bills influence the customer's perception of a business and whether they will deal with the business in the future. Furthermore, customers expect a business to recognize and remember them regardless of how they interact with the company. As such, customer service representatives and others who interact with customers at a given touch point have to be able to access historical data about the customer. Such data includes every customer interaction with the business through every other touch point.

For example, within the CRM system for American Express, the agents who handle flight changes for customers must have access to airline, hotel, and car rental data in order to better serve the customer and to ensure that the customer uses an AMEX card to pay for the services. Customers expect a business to provide the same service through every touch point. If they interact with a business through the Web, for example, they expect to be able to verify the status of an order placed on the telephone or in person.

Relationship Dynamics

The interaction between Hank and Paul illustrates the complexity of relationship dynamics in a typical customer-company relationship. For example, both Paul and Hank are dealing with several known and unknown resource investments.

From Paul's perspective, he has invested time in getting to know Hank, his company, and in exploring the future service that Hank is likely to provide. Compared to the Web-based bike outlets, Hank's bike shop represents a relatively known quantity. Looking for an online bike dealer or another bike shop in town represents an unknown that may turn out to provide better prices or service but will definitely require an additional investment in Paul's time and energy. The dynamics of the relationship between Paul and Hank, from Paul's perspective, can be summed up as "the fear of loss is greater than the prospect for gain." In other words, Paul has a known quantity in Hank, given his investment in time. Paul can go on to look for another bike shop but may turn up nothing better, and lose time in the process.

From Hank's perspective, Paul represents an ideal customer and one worth taking care of. Hank knows that attracting and establishing new customers costs money and that it's much cheaper to turn an existing customer into a repeat customer than to search for a new customer. Paul is young, active, and, based on Hank's dealing with customers with similar profiles in the past, likely to buy several accessories for his new bike as he becomes more comfortable with it. From Hank's perspective, the dynamics of the relationship can be summed up as "the cost of retaining a customer is less than the cost of recruiting another one."

Hank assumes that Paul will likely buy fenders for wet-weather riding, riding apparel for hot and cold weather, biking shoes with cleats for better control on his off-road adventures, and perhaps a spare tire, a bike pump, and a roadside toolkit. In addition, Hank knows that most of his business is through word of mouth and that if he takes care of Paul, it's likely to mean business from other students as well. In addition, from a practical perspective, Paul's apartment is only a few blocks from the bike shop, and the five minutes it takes Hank to deliver and pick up Paul's bike doesn't significantly cost time.

It helps the relationship that Hank is genuine—he's genuinely into bikes, he genuinely likes people, and he genuinely likes Paul and wants Paul to be happy with his purchase. In addition, Paul can sense this. As a result, the relationship is much stronger than one based solely on business profit and loss.

Loyalty Effect

When it came time for Paul to add an accessory to his bicycle, he considered going through a mail-order catalog because it offered the panniers at a considerable price savings; however, Paul changed his mind and purchased the accessory from Hank because he was so impressed with the customer service that Hank provided. In other words, Paul's behavior was consistent with that of a loyal customer; it was based more on emotion and feeling than on logic. There was no logical reason for Paul to spend more money to get the same pannier that he could have bought from the mail-order catalog.

From a practical perspective, it's impossible to predict which customers are loyal and which ones aren't. Loyalty, like love or loathing, is impossible to quantify exactly. What can be quantified is customer behavior, and where customer loyalty is concerned, the closest factor that can be measured is customer behavior. The Loyalty Effect provides a model that can be used to predict customer behavior, based on factors that positively and negatively affect behaviors associated with loyalty—positive referrals, repeat business, and continuing a business relationship even when potentially superior competing products and services are available.

FIGURE 2-3

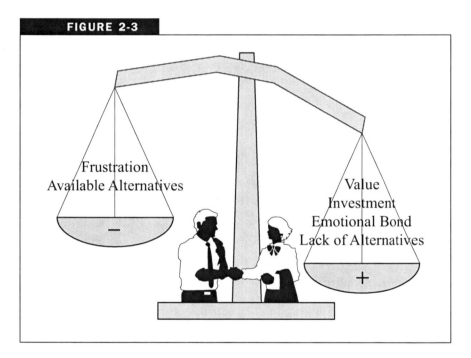

Figure 2-3 shows that the positive contributors to behaviors consistent with loyalty include:

- *Value.* The greater the perceived value of a company's goods or services, the greater the Loyalty Effect. Customers expect value for their money.

- *Investment.* The more time, energy, or money invested in a relationship, the more likely the relationship will continue.

The more time Paul spends with Hank and his bike shop, the more likely Paul will continue to do business with Hank, even if it costs more to do so.

- *Difficulty Locating Alternatives.* The more unique or readily available a product or service, the more likely a customer will continue buying it from a particular company. Hank provides a unique service that's responsive in part because it's so close to his apartment.

- *A Positive Emotional Bond.* A personal, emotional bond with a company representative is often the most important factor in creating a loyal customer. People don't normally form bonds with companies, but with other people. Paul doesn't care about the factory workers who assembled his bike in Taiwan, but he does care for Hank's welfare.

Negative contributors to loyalty behaviors include:

- *Number of Affordable Alternatives.* The more affordable alternatives exist, the less the Loyalty Effect. All else being equal, geographic proximity counts for a lot. In Paul's case, one of the big draws of Hank's bike shop is that it is virtually in walking distance from his apartment. If there were two other bike shops in Paul's neighborhood, there would be less of a Loyalty Effect between Paul and Hank's shop.

- *Customer Frustration.* Nothing poisons an otherwise ideal business relationship more than customer frustration. Being put on hold, corralled into endless push-button menus and an extended-hold customer support system, having to wait in excessively long lines, and similar forms of customer torture can quickly end an otherwise ideal customer–company relationship. Paul's inability to contact the online bike shop by phone is an example of how customer frustration can put an end to any form of relationship.

The Loyalty Effect model shows how customer behavior can be influenced—either to continue the relationship or to terminate it— depending on what elements in the model are stressed. For example, customers can be intentionally dissuaded from doing business with a company by adding a frustration element to their interaction. Putting certain customers on extended holds when they call for support, delay- ing or failing to respond to written or E-mail messages, and, in a retail setting, ignoring some customers while attending to others are all methods guaranteed to make customers think twice about continuing to do business with the company.

FIGURE 2-4

Reps	Customers	Category
	10	Profitable
	1,000	Neutral
	20,000	Unprofitable

The typical customer support pyramids, shown in Figure 2-4, illus- trate how many companies are affecting customer behavior by control- ling their frustration level. For example, an investment firm might assign one customer service representative to every 10 of its most profitable customers (i.e., customers responsible for more than 100,000 of revenue per year). With this ratio of representatives to customer support, the goal may be that phone calls are answered within five or six rings.

At the other extreme, the tens of thousands of customers who are costing the company money, either because their account balances are too low to cover the cost of their monthly statements or because they trade, say, less than once a year, might be assigned only one representative per four thousand customers. They can expect to be put on hold for a half hour or more, listening to "your call is important to us" recorded messages.

In the middle of the spectrum, the one thousand revenue-neutral customers (i.e., customers who neither make money for the company nor cost it money) might be assigned one representative per five hundred customers; however, some of these customers may become profitable in the future. For example, Paul may fit into the revenue-neutral category now, but once he graduates and becomes established, he may become a profitable customer. The customers in the middle category might have to put up with being on hold for three to five minutes before being attended to.

There may be legal constraints associated with exactly what methods can be used to dissuade customer interactions. The decision about which customers should be given less than first-class treatment can't be based on sex, race, or religion, for example. It is acceptable, however, to use automatic customer ID technologies that look up a caller's status with the company, based on their account number, for example, and to automatically categorize them in terms of profitability. For example, the system in a bank might automatically categorize customers based on their credit risk. The system could consider the number of late and defaulted payments over the last seven or ten years, the customer's occupation, annual income, and similar factors.

With enough peripheral information, it's possible to ascertain sex, race, and religion to circumvent legal concerns. For example, minorities and women tend to make less money in certain jobs than do their white and male counterparts.

Summary

From the customer's perspective, CRM is about good (i.e., affordable, reliable, personable, truthful, and responsive) customer service. The customer that a company wants to hold onto, who will remain loyal, and bring his or her business to the company, is worth the trouble of paying for a good CRM system, not a frustrating one.

Customers develop expectations based on information gained from a company's touch points, including the brand identity as promoted in the media, personal interactions, E-mail, mail, phone, and other lines of communications. The relationship dynamics of customer-company interactions are a function of the resources invested in the ongoing relationship, as well as the other options available. The Loyalty Effect provides a model that can be used to predict and affect customer behavior, in terms of increased or decreased customer-company interactions.

The way to love anything is to realize that it may be lost.

G.K. Chesterton

CHAPTER 3

The Corporation

After reading this chapter you will be able to

- Appreciate customer relationship management from the corporation's perspective

- Understand the significance of taking a comprehensive view of the customer

- Understand the importance of internal processes in the customer relationship, including the way products and services are developed

- Recongnize the need for the corporation to stay within its area of core competency when attempting to offer the customer increased value

- Understand how employee satisfaction affects the relationship with customers

- Appreciate the significance of strategic partnerships and alliances

- Recongnize the need for constant innovation because of rising customer expectations

CRM is about the relationship between customer and companies, with each contributing to and receiving something from the relationship. Whereas customers expect value for their money, companies expect money and often a degree of loyalty in exchange for their goods and services. The challenge, from the corporate perspective, is to provide customers with value that meets their expectations and gain the revenue from the relationship that the company expects, with minimal disruption to the internal processes of the company. In every lasting relationship, it's important for each side to understand what the other side wants and needs. Chapter 2 noted that the value of the relationship from the customer's perspective is a function of the market value of the goods and services offered by the company. In addition, the emotional value of the brand to the customer and the offerings of the competition also affect how the customer values the relationship. In particular, a competitor can undercut the price of a comparable product or service, thereby lowering the perceived value of the product or service offered by the first company.

From the company's perspective, an ongoing relationship with the customer has a cost, regardless of whether the relationship is profitable or not. There is the cost of doing business, which normally includes customer support. There is also lost opportunity cost because corporate resources may be used on one group of customers at the expense of another group. The cost also involves the ongoing task of gathering and sorting data to determine what can and should be offered to the customer in exchange for repeat business. To illustrate these and other concepts, let's continue with the story of the roommates.

Extended Family

Jen, Paul's roommate, noticed how much fun Paul was having biking with his new friend. She asked about his bike, how much it cost, and where he bought it, thinking that biking might be something she and her boyfriend Bob could do together on weekends. After all, Bob had a bike that he occasionally rode to work. Jen bought a bike from Hank about five years ago, but the bike has been in storage for more than a year.

The following weekend, Jen and Paul took her bike to the bike shop to ask Hank what would be involved in getting it back into shape. Hank spent five minutes going over the bike, noting the cracked tires, frayed cables, rusted chain, and other points of disrepair, and gave her a quote for the work. He noted that, because she bought the bike from him, the price was discounted considerably from what he would normally charge. Jen agreed to the charges and made arrangements to pick up the bike later that week.

In his conversation with Jen, Hank asked what she planned to do with the bike, why the sudden interest in biking, and her longer-term plans. When Hank learned of the planned biking trips with her boyfriend, he offered to take a look at his bike as well, extending the same discount to any repairs that might be needed.

After Paul and Jen left, Hank took out a new index card and updated Jen's record—Hank maintained an index card file on all of the shop's customers over the past decade—and handed it to his two assistants to file. He noted the types of repairs that he was going to make on the bike, Jen's riding habits, and her relationship with Bob, and that he had extended customer benefits to Bob.

A few days later, Bob stopped by with Jen to pick up her bike and to have Hank check out Bob's bike. After a quick going-over, Hank discovered that several braze-ons—the points of attachment for fenders, water bottle, and panniers—were cracked. The braze-ons were repairable, and the bike was otherwise structurally sound, but Hank didn't feel confident about his ability to do the work. He told Bob about a larger bike shop across town that specialized in custom frame work. Otherwise, Hank offered to replace the chain and one of Bob's tires.

Bob thanked Hank and said that he might as well have the other bike shop do the repair work as well, given that he'd have to bring the bike there anyway. Hank gave Bob his business card, and asked him to call if he had any problems with the bike anyway. Hank took out another 3x5 card and created a record for Bob, noting the model and condition of his bike, gave the card to one of his assistants to file, and began work on another bike.

Corporate Perspective

CRM from the corporate perspective is primarily about creating a positive experience for profitable customers. For example, in the story, in which Hank plays the role of the corporation, Hank creates a positive experience for Jen by extending her customer discount to include Bob. This positive experience can come about by increasing customer value either for all customers or for only a target group of customers. Revisiting the definition of CRM, we find that the key concepts from the corporate perspective are mutually beneficial commercial exchanges and profitability. The key goals are to keep the customer's business and to dissuade the customer from participating in exchanges that are unprofitable to the company.

Treating all customers as valued customers has the advantage of simplicity. There is no need to create customer profiles, track customer activity over time, or hire marketing consultants to discover which customers are profitable and which are not. The disadvantage is that increasing customer value globally may be wasting a significant amount of corporate resources, depending on the marginal cost of increasing customer value and the ratio of profitable to unprofitable customers. If most customers are profitable and the marginal cost of increasing customer value by increasing customer support by, say 20 percent, is insignificant, then targeting specific customers may not be worth the effort.

If 80 percent of profits are derived from the top 20 percent of the customers, however, then identifying the top 20 percent of customers may be critical to the success of the company. One industry that follows the so-called 80/20 rule of profitability is brokerage services. Heavy, frequent traders, represented by large corporations and wealthy investors, are the bulk of commissions, compared to much smaller private traders who might trade relatively small amounts of stock once a year or less. Targeting actions that increase customer value to the profitable customers is especially important if the marginal cost of the added value is high. That is, the need for targeting added value to specific customers is inversely related to the percentage of profitable customers (see Figure 3-1).

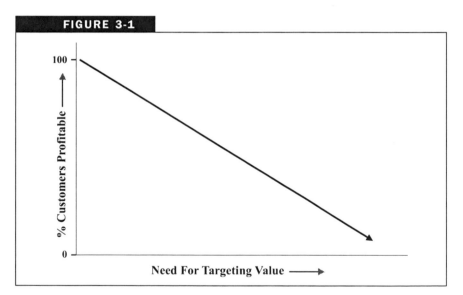

FIGURE 3-1

As discussed in Chapter 2, one way to increase profitability is to provide customer service in proportion to customer profitability. The greater the profitability of a group, the more responsive customer service should be to its needs. In this regard, the idea of running a quality, profitable business is not simply to give customers everything they want, but the goal, from a corporate perspective, has to be to improve or at least maintain the bottom line.

In the story of the bike shop, Hank extends Jen's customer discount to her boyfriend, Bob. This gesture not only enhances Hank's relationship with Jen, but it might also make Bob a customer. Assuming the marginal cost of extending the discount to Bob is minimal, Hank is increasing the value of his relationship to Jen, whether or not Bob accepts the offer.

Comprehensive View of the Customer

Not all customer relationships are as easily managed as the one between Hank and Jen in the story; however, even in this simple case, Hank has to invest time in getting to know Jen. He determines why Jen bikes, her other exercise habits, her goals and aspirations regarding biking, and other peripheral factors in her life, such as Bob, that may influence her buying habits in the future.

Focusing on the customer warrants revisiting the concept of touch points. A comprehensive or 360-degree view of customers includes

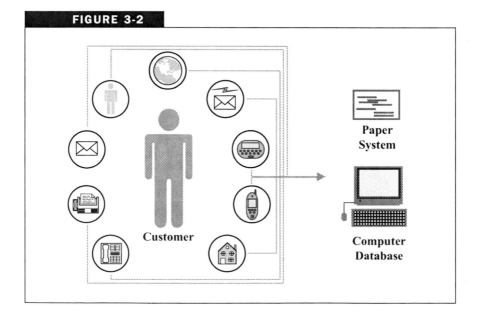

FIGURE 3-2

information that is collected at each of the company's touch points (see Figure 3-2). The difference in touch points from a business rather than a customer perspective is the focus on data collection and management, not simply communicating with the customer. Note that the media touch point is not shown in the figure because radio, TV, and newspaper advertisements aren't yet interactive and so don't allow collection of customer data. Regardless of the touch points involved, the data can be stored and managed on index cards or, if the quantity of data and the economics allow it, in a computer system. As discussed further in Chapter 6, the computer provides several advantages over an index card system, including the ability to ask questions quickly and to generate lists of customers by age, product manufacturer, original purchase date, and other criteria that can be useful in customer support.

Processing customer information obtained through the touch points is complex, in part because there are so many customers. Although a customer integrates all of the information instantly, from the corporate perspective, data from all customers must be collected, verified, and formally analyzed before it is useful for making decisions.

Whereas customers derive some sense of value, satisfaction, and loyalty through interacting with the touch points, from a corporate perspective, the goal is crafting a comprehensive view of the customer. In this regard, the first and most important thing to know about customers is whether they are a current or potential source of revenue in excess of expenses or if the customer represents a continual loss for the company. If a customer is expected to remain unprofitable for the duration of the relationship, then the corporation has no motivation to continue the relationship past its contractual obligations and no need to gather more customer information. The only thing that is of economic value about the customer is the knowledge that he or she is unprofitable, and renewing the relationship in the future should be reconsidered.

If a customer is profitable, however, or has a likelihood of becoming profitable in the immediate future, then five kinds of additional information should be gathered, including customer wants and needs, the customer purchase cycle, customer interaction opportunities, a customer profile, and a customer life cycle, as described as follows.

Customer Wants and Needs

From the perspective of CRM, all customers have wants and needs that they look to the company to satisfy. In this context, needs are defined as the prerequisites that qualify customers to use a company's goods and/or services. The customer who purchases a peripheral for his or her computer, only to discover that the software driver doesn't work with the installed version of the operating system, needs the appropriate software from the company. Without the software upgrade, the customer won't be able to use the peripheral and may return the product for a refund.

Wants, in this context, are defined as desirable products and services. This isn't to say that customers' wants are necessarily less important from their perspective; most customers base their purchase decisions on wants, not needs. Few people need a new computer, flashy automobile, or fancy suit, but thanks to marketing efforts, potential customers want many things. Customers may want personal, immediate customer service, for example, because they are accustomed to a high level of service. In many cases, these customers are also willing to pay extra for the extra services—whether it's the privileges associated with carrying a certain charge card or a membership card in a mail-order, online, or retail store. American Express, Road Runner Sports, Performance, and other nationally recognized brands manage to package their customer services in a way that customers are happy to pay for them.

It's important for a corporation to know or accurately predict its customers' needs so that it can prepare to address them. In the story, Jen brings her bike to Hank's shop to be repaired. Given the age of her bike, Hank predicts that she will need a new bike within a year or two. Similarly, Bob needs to have his braze-ons repaired, something that Hank is ill-equipped to do. That is, in establishing his business, he either purposely decided not to offer bike frame repairs or he predicted that too few customers would need the service to make it worth the investment in equipment and training. Perhaps his initial assessment was based on the quality of bicycles manufactured a decade ago, and overall quality has declined since then, creating more of a demand for frame work.

Looking to the future, Hank can predict Bob and Jen's need for winter riding apparel as cold weather approaches and can proactively send Bob and Jen a brochure on winter riding specials. Similarly, in one year, when Jen's bike is likely to be in need of an overhaul, Hank can send a card to Jen to remind her of his service. Note that Hank could have simply installed a new tire and chains on Bob's bike and ignored the problems with the braze-ons, but he did not do that because of his business ethics.

Customer Purchase Cycle

One of the criteria in evaluating the value a customer presents for future business is the customer purchase cycle—the time between a customer's repeat purchase of good and services. The frequency and likelihood of additional purchases as well as the nature of those purchases depend on both the customer and the product. An avid cyclist involved in racing might be in the market for a new frame every two or three years and accessories every few months. By contrast, a weekend cyclist might own the same bike and components for a decade or more before buying a second bike and accessories.

Continuing with the story, assuming Jen continues to ride her bike, she will probably decide to buy a new, lighter bike within the next year.

She may take six months or more to save the money for a new bike. Given that her bike is about five years old, her purchase cycle is about six-and-a-half years.

Customer Interaction Opportunities

To capitalize on repeat business and enhance customer loyalty, companies should explore the costs and benefits of all customer interactions. In this regard, certain types of customers favor some touch points over others. Not everyone has a fax, for example, and those who do often don't appreciate flyers printed at their cost. By contrast, enthusiasts of all sorts, from golfers to scuba divers, have their own magazine and trade journals that companies can use to maintain a connection with their customers.

Many customers prefer brochures or simply a Web site that they can visit instead of receiving a phone call in the middle of dinner. In Jen's case, a flyer announcing sales on new bicycle models, mailed quarterly, would probably be appreciated most. A personal letter from Hank might be appropriate in a year, when she's contemplating a new bike purchase; however, if Hank were trying to solicit business from Paul's girlfriend, Julie, the avid mountain biker, he might consider hosting a mountain bike competition.

Customer Profile

In order for a company to allocate its customer support resources most effectively, the company needs to know as much relevant information about the customer as possible. The customer profile can be limited to demographic information, such as name, address, contact information, and product or service purchase history. This level of detail may be sufficient for some purposes, such as contacting customers who may have purchased an older model widget to inform them of a much-improved one; however, the ideal profile may include additional information, such as birth date, education level, family and marital status, hobbies and special interests, occupation, membership in special organizations, lifestyle, and vacation habits.

Some information may be industry-specific. A software company that produces, say, utilities for programmers, would be interested to know a programmer's area of expertise, the programming languages, the hardware platform, operating system, and any other third-party software products that he or she uses on a regular basis. This information would be valuable in determining whether announcements of new utilities would likely be of interest to the programmer. Similarly, an insurance company would likely be concerned with a customer's current income, net worth, real estate holdings, and number of dependents in determining whether it can offer customers additional services—increased life insurance coverage, for example, if the customer's number of dependents has increased since the original insurance policies were drawn up.

By engaging in a conversation with Jen, Hank was able to determine why she had suddenly become interested in biking, and from that information, could serve her better. He could also better estimate the profitability of an ongoing relationship. Similarly, many magazines regularly poll readers to determine which articles are most interesting, as well as their involvement with their own company, from their position and responsibilities to their annual budget.

Customer Life Cycle

The fifth and final major area of information that the company should gather is the customer life cycle. In many respects, the customer life cycle, which includes the life events of the typical customer, parallels the typical product life cycle, which moves from introduction and growth to maturity and finally decline. By accurately predicting the life cycle of its customers, a company can proactively offer appropriate products and services to its existing customer to extend the company-customer relationship. For example, by examining the customer's life cycle, a financial institution can send customers information on auto loans at 25, life insurance at 30, mortgage information at 35, and retirement funds at 55.

In the story, Hank predicts—based on his experience with bike shop customers over the past two decades—that as Jen and Bob age, they'll spend less time on off-road cycling and eventually put the bikes away as children and other responsibilities come along. He also predicts that when their children are age two or so, they'll be back to purchase infant seats for their bikes, so that their toddlers can ride with them.

Segmentation

The rationale for going through the trouble and expense of gathering and predicting customer behavior is to segment customers into groups of likely behavior. For example, the company will find it advantageous to define which group of customers will likely require or request service for their bicycle, house, or car in the next six months. Segmentation is especially useful in allocating limited corporate resources, such as customer service representative time, and identifying customers who may be willing to pay for extra service. For example, many corporations offer special service options, in the form of club memberships, that allow customers in need of help to get it, without charging customers who don't need help. Segmentation is also used in marketing campaigns to define a target audience within a group of customers, such as which insurance policy-holders might be interested in additional forms of insurance.

Although segmentation is much easier with computer-based tools, it has been practiced for decades with index card systems. The advantage of computer-based segmentation is that ad hoc questions, such as the number of customers above a certain age who haven't yet purchased a mortgage in a given area, can be answered rapidly.

The disadvantage of automated (computer-based) methods of segmentation is the cost of gathering information, increased complexity, and potentially limited return on investment, which is discussed further in Chapter 7. Regardless of the methods used to gather and manage customer data, the cost of gathering data has to be weighed against the likelihood of profit from these customers. Spending five dollars for a comprehensive customer profile may make sense for customers who are likely to purchase a second Porsche in the next six months, but not for customers who may buy a spare tire during the same six-month period.

Internal Processes

By determining which customers should be treated with first-class service and which ones should be given economy-class service, a company can save on the cost of customer support. But savings can also come about through increased effectiveness of a corporation's internal processes. The internal processes, from the manner in which products are developed to the way in which service is allocated to customers, eventually affect the efficiency, effectiveness, and the return on investment (ROI) of a CRM initiative.

Mass-produced customization is one means of increasing the value of the customer relationship. Mass customization comes about through the modification and improvement of internal processes. In this approach, products and services are developed in a way that lets them fit the needs of the customer more closely. Mass customization is commonly applied to cars (custom interior and exterior color combinations), cell phones (custom covers), pagers (custom colors), hamburgers (the "have it your way" campaign by Burger King), and to the dismay of business travelers, even airline tickets. Business travelers and vacationers negotiate with the airlines for travel services that are custom priced at what the business travel market will bear. Unfortunately for the business traveler, the added price of a ticket over what a vacation traveler pays isn't associated with any additional service.

Mass customization, when implemented over an existing process, may not be economically feasible. For example, modifying a bicycle assembly line so that different color frames can be matched with specific components may require a complete process overhaul and one that results in a product with a high marginal cost. That is, the added cost for each bicycle produced through the mass customization approach may be so expensive that the product would not be competitive in the marketplace.

If the process of mass customization with an eye toward future CRM is built into the manufacturing process from the start, however, as Dell Computer does with its line of laptop and desktop computers, then the marginal cost can be contained while providing customers with a product that better suits their needs. For example, customers can go to the Dell Web site or speak to a sales representative on the phone and configure a laptop with the RAM, hard disk, CPU, and accessories that exactly suit their needs and budget. A machine with those specifications will be produced by the automated factory within about two weeks.

More important, from a CRM perspective, Dell tracks the laptop and the customer in its database. When a customer contacts Dell for a memory, operating system, or hardware upgrade, the customer service representative has access to the exact hardware configuration the customer is using and ensures that the hardware and software are compatible.

Dell's internal processes are also configured so that the company can act proactively, warning customers of potential problems with software and hardware. For example, when Microsoft Windows 2000 was released, many Dell computers (and computers from other vendors as well) could not use the operating system without upgrading the software drivers to the CD-ROM drives and other peripheral hardware. Instead of waiting to hear from customers with problems, Dell proactively contacted each customer and told them of an area on their Web site dedicated to solving Windows 2000 problems, saving many calls to customer support.

FIGURE 3-3

amazon.com.

We'll be right back!

We're sorry, but our store is closed temporarily. We expect to be back soon. If you would like to be notified when we reopen, please leave your e-mail address below and we will be happy to let you know.

Per our Site Availability Policy, if this closure lasts longer than 30 minutes, but less than or equal to 2 hours, all auctions scheduled to end during the closure period will be extended by at least twice the amount of the time closed. If the closure lasts longer than 2 hours, all auctions scheduled to end during the closure period will be extended by 24 hours.

Again, we apologize for the inconvenience, and thank you for your patience.

Your friends at Amazon.com

Please enter your e-mail address: [_____] [Submit]

Similarly, Amazon.com's internal processes recognize that connectivity problems are inevitable. The company acts to proactively address the most common customer complaints and questions. One of these is disruption of service, which not only costs Amazon.com money from lost sales, but may also disrupt time-sensitive offers, such as auctions. Having an internal process that makes allowances for inevitable outages and proactively addresses remedies alleviates messages to and from customer service (see Figure 3-3). Note that this remedy treats all customers equally—from frequent users to first-time users alike. In other words, CRM is built into the internal process of the company; it's not an exception or a means of putting out fires as they arise in the organization.

The effect of internal processes optimization on CRM extends to how customer data are gathered, managed, and ultimately used. In Hank's case, he creates the customer profile index cards, which are then filed by one of his assistants. Depending on the number of cards and the number of items tracked in Hank's filing system, it may be cost and time effective to move to a computer-based system. It may also pay to assign one of his existing workers, or hire an office assistant, to manage the customer database and other administrative chores; however, instituting these changes will not only change the normal internal processes of Hank's business, but may change the way employees feel about their jobs as well.

Related to the optimization of internal processes, it's important to consider the company's core competency, so that the competency is enhanced, not weakened. Other factors relevant to core competency are described as follows.

Core Competency

In maximizing customer value—and company revenue—many companies are tempted to stray from their area of core competency. Although there's always an attraction to stretch a little to take advantage of additional revenue, straying from the corporate core competency brings with it inefficiencies and diversion of resources that could otherwise be applied to work in the area of competency.

In a rapidly shifting market, it may be necessary to diversify customer service offerings to suit the needs of customers, but even diversification should be done with the core competency in mind. For Hank to do the braze-on work, he would have to invest in new equipment, learn to use it, and manage to pay for it somehow. Because the bike shop that he referred Bob to specialized in modifying frames, their mechanics can probably offer a better product at cheaper prices than

Hank, even if he did invest in the equipment, simply because of their expertise and higher volume.

Hank elected to send the brazing work to a competing bike shop because that type of work was outside his core competency. His core competencies lie in customer relationship management, fitting frames to customers, overhauling bikes, and other mechanical tasks. Although Hank was tempted to take on the work, especially because Bob would likely purchase accessories in the near future, he didn't want to deliver a product that he couldn't guarantee. A failed attempt to repair Bob's bike might have negatively affected Hank's relationship with Jen, who was likely to buy accessories and eventually a new bike.

Few companies are large enough or have deep enough pockets to simultaneously extend their core competency in multiple directions. Microsoft is one notable exception. Few companies have the resources to simultaneously develop operating system software, game software, office telephone systems, and, most recently, high-end game hardware. Most successful companies focus on and excel at one thing. For example, although Mercedes-Benz produces a bicycle, most of its production, marketing, and customer support efforts are focused on creating cars that are fun to drive.

One of the core competencies of successful companies is knowing how to keep employees happy, motivated, and productive. As discussed in the following section, where CRM is concerned, whoever answers the phone for customer support must be satisfied and proud of his or her job and company.

Employee Satisfaction

It's difficult for customer service representatives to make customers feel good about their company if they're dissatisfied as employees; however, numerous challenges are associated with working with customer service representatives. Not only do they tend to be the least paid, least trained employees in a company, but customer service representatives also have the highest attrition rate. In addition, many customer service representatives view their jobs as a temporary position while they're attending school or saving money until they can find a better job. The representatives who do stay around for a year or more often end up as managers, removed from direct customer contact. As a result, customers often deal with employees who may not have "bought into" the corporate vision. In addition, they may not know the product and its problems or solutions very well. Instead of direct experience, they may have to work with problem-solution databases, which transforms the training of a customer representative from knowing solutions to knowing how to look them up. This situation also shifts the cost from training to establishing and maintaining the database. In the end, relying on problem-solution databases is like hiring a team of vegetarians to staff the tables at a steakhouse —customers will likely sense that the staff's heart isn't in their product.

Enhancing employee satisfaction and a sense of connectedness with the company doesn't mean giving customer service representatives free run of the company. After all, customer service representatives have access to the most sensitive data in the company—from the problems with the company's products and services to the identity and relationship history of each customer. As such, an increasing problem with some customer service representatives—and employees in general—is that of taking customer data with them to use for their own purposes, such as using customer data for mailings for their side businesses. Part of the problem stems from computerization of customer service. Computers make the process of taking thousands of company contacts as easy as inserting a floppy disk in a computer and copying files onto it.

Creating a cadre of satisfied customer service representatives involves treating them with an appropriate level of respect, which they extend

Increasing Employee Satisfaction

The high employee turnover in most customer support departments need not be a forgone conclusion. Steps that can be taken to increase retention and performance include:

- Offering promotion opportunities within the customer support department as well as transfers to other departments.

- Establishing recognition awards for quantifiable performance, such as number of problems resolved per week.

- Including customer support representatives in product roll-outs and other corporate events that could benefit from representative buy-in.

- Including customer service representatives in product announcements and corporate newsletters.

Recognition and a sense of team membership help increase employee satisfaction, especially for employees who aren't normally considered in high-profile positions, such as customer service representatives.

Consider how the U.S. Air Force increased retention, job performance, and overall job satisfaction for low-level jet fighter support crew personnel by increasing their visibility through a public relations campaign. In addition, the Air Force had photos taken of each support crew team in front of their jet fighter, with the pilot and other crew in the background, to give the support crew a sense of ownership and importance in the overall operation. In the past, the pilot took center stage and the support crew was relegated to the background. Everyone needs to feel appreciated.

to customers. Other obvious techniques, such as providing representatives with the appropriate monetary incentives, recognition for a job well done, a way to communicate with more technically knowledgeable employees, and a career growth path can help create employee satisfaction; however, simply paying employees more doesn't solve the long-term challenges of retention. A fun work environment, training, and opportunities to provide excellent service—the type of work environment popularized by Nordstrom—when properly implemented, result in a win–win situation for customers and employees.

The challenge, from an ROI perspective, is to rationalize the cost of hiring internal customer service representatives when these jobs could be outsourced to competent, highly skilled, and inexpensive representatives working in huge call centers in the Midwest, Florida, and, increasingly, India. These outsourced employees, even if they do provide an enhanced revenue, may not have the same level of enthusiasm as representatives who work within the company; however, outsourcing CRM and forming other strategic partnerships and alliances is a fact of modern corporate life.

Outsourcing is a challenge because customer service representatives have data important to all areas of the company. They are the first to know of customer problems, and they are supposed to communicate solutions and workarounds to customers as soon as they are available. As such, customer service representatives have to be able to communicate with engineers, developers, and others involved in creating and delivering the product or service. When a customer service representative is off-site, the engineers and others involved in finding a solution to a customer problem are one more level removed from direct interaction with the customer.

As such, in addition to cost savings, the criteria for outsourcing CRM functions should include provisions for a mechanism whereby new problems can be escalated directly to engineering or product development in the company. This arrangement is usually accomplished by a technical liaison on the CRM service provider's side who is knowledgeable about the company and its products, as well as the development staff.

Another obvious criteria for identifying an appropriate company to outsource CRM activities is the general area of customer service representative expertise. For example, a company that specializes in providing CRM for software products would likely do a better job at supporting another software package rather than a CRM firm that services a variety of areas.

If a company's products and services are used worldwide, then an obvious benefit to outsourcing CRM is that country-, language-, and time-specific support can be provided more effectively by a local company. A CRM service company that operates out of Germany, for example, is probably better able to service customers in Germany, compared to a U.S. firm hiring German-speaking representatives in the United States.

Strategic Partnerships and Alliances

Customers are always looking for more value for their money. One way that companies can provide enhanced value—and realize greater profitability—is by bundling the company's products and services with those of complementary companies through a variety of partnerships and strategic alliances. One of the most visible strategic alliances is between the charge card companies and airlines, rental car, mail-order companies, and hotel chains, where air miles are given for charges made through specific companies. For example, the American Express–Delta Skymiles program incorporates several strategic alliances, including one with Delta Airlines, The Sharper Image, Eddie Bauer, Avis car rental, the Hyatt, Sheraton, and Westin hotel chains, and Renaissance Cruises. American Express has also joined with Blockbuster, Compaq, Hertz, and Vail Resorts to form e-Rewards, a program that provides gifts to customers who agree to receive E-mail from a variety of companies. Similarly, Bass Hotels & Resorts in Latin America is offering miles on American, United, Delta, Continental, and British Airways.

Strategic partnerships and alliances within the scope of CRM generally fall into one of five categories:

1. *Intelligence.* These companies provide trend and market analysis, survey results, and information on what the competition is up to. Business intelligence is especially important in estimating customer expectations, which in turn affects the level of service the company should offer at a given price. If the competition is offering 24/7 phone-in support for one year after the sale of a comparably priced product, then the company has to consider matching that level of service or comparably increasing the value of its offerings in some other way, such as by doubling the current business-hours-only phone-in support from one year to two years after the sale.

2. *Marketing.* These companies create advertising campaigns, slogans, corporate logos, messages, and manage promotions. Marketing has a role in managing customer expectations, in terms of quality, support, and value.

3. *Sales.* These companies create catalogs, customer needs analysis, and ordering. For example, catalogs that target particular customer populations can be cost-effective means of reaching a much larger customer base. From a CRM perspective, strategic partnerships and alliances in the area of sales can free up employees to support customers. In addition, customer needs analysis may be directly applicable to an internal or external CRM effort.

4. *Service.* These companies specialize in employee and customer training and support. As mentioned previously, outsourcing customer service is an increasingly popular cost-cutting exercise for many companies. The challenge in using one of the call center warehouses—a building full of telephone operators, each of whom may be trained to handle calls from up to 10 or more products from different companies—is the depth of understanding of any particular product and the lack of loyalty to the company supplying the product. To one of these warehouse operators, a problem with a widget from one company is the same as a problem from any other company with a similar widget. The attitude of a customer service representative working within a company can be different. A representative who has actually seen and used the product, who has interacted with people within the company, and, most importantly, who has a financial stake in the company (such as through stock options and bonuses based on the level of service provided) often makes an extra effort to understand and solve the customers' problems.

5. *Technology.* These companies offer databases, software, and processes that can streamline internal and external CRM operations. Hundreds of companies produce database software and computer hardware designed to create a collaborative environment to support better CRM, some of which actually work as advertised when implemented properly. The relevance of these and other technologies to CRM is discussed in detail in Chapter 4.

Part of the motivation for looking to strategic partnerships and alliances is economic, and part is to free up internal resources so that the company can respond to the constant change in the marketplace. As described as follows, constant innovation is critical at a time of increasing customer expectations, smaller margins, and global competition.

IN THE REAL WORLD

Offshore Support

Since its inception in Jeff Bezos' garage, Amazon has been the standard by which all other dotCom companies measure the quality of their customer service. At one time, Amazon had nearly 400 full-time customer service representatives in the United States handling predominantly E-mail from customers. With the downturn of the U.S. economy and pressure from Wall Street to turn a profit, however, Amazon has resorted to using offshore customer service representatives in India and elsewhere. Customers calling or, more often, e-mailing Amazon for support have no way of knowing where customer service representatives are working.

Because customer service representatives need only a telephone and a computer that is connected to the company's network, more companies, including Fortune 500 companies such as Hewlett-Packard, are allowing customer service representatives to work from home.

Constant Innovation

Every CEO has heard the mantra that the only constant in today's economy is change. When it comes to CRM, change—in the positive direction—is a prerequisite to ongoing success. Customer expectations are increasing, fueled by global competition, the efficiency of the Internet, and the ability to compare wholesale and retail prices on the Web. The globalization of customer service is a phenomenon that has happened in the last few years. In other words, it's difficult to hide information from customers. In a few mouse clicks, an Internet-savvy customer can check a company's profit margins, its volume of sales listed on the last annual report, the companies that produce the major competing products, and a review of the company's products and services, including customer support.

Given this environment, there is constant pressure for innovation. Consider, for example, how Amazon.com has evolved from an online bookstore to a personalized book and product referral service. Customers who visit Amazon.com are greeted by name; they can track their outstanding orders and other account information; and they can even elect to be notified if an item they're looking for becomes available. Similarly, FedEx evolved its phone-in customer service to allow customers to track packages at any time from the Web. Not only did FedEx increase the perceived value of its service, but it reduced the need for customer service representatives as well.

Domino's Pizza—really a delivery service that happens to transport pizza pies—became a success in the saturated takeout pizza market through constant innovation of its delivery service, not by changing its pizza recipes. The company developed special packaging to maintain the quality of the product longer, guaranteed delivery within a time limit, and created an internal process that supported consistent production and delivery of pizzas. These measures allow the company to consistently deliver what it promises. Regardless of what a company produces, great CRM begins with delivering on promises; even the best customer service won't make up for product that doesn't perform as promised.

Summary

From the corporate perspective, CRM is a balancing act—managing often increasing customer expectations while delivering value in line with what is profitable for the corporation. To do so requires information, not only about the customer, but also about the competition. In creating additional value for the customer, there is a temptation to stray from the core competency of the corporation, but doing so without attention to the internal processes of the organization can be detrimental. When it comes to delivering customer service, employee satisfaction of the front-line customer service representatives is reflected directly in the way they handle customer complaints. Strategic partnerships and alliances often make it possible to direct limited corporate resources to CRM initiatives, or, conversely, to outsource customer support and other CRM functions. Regardless of the strategy used to implement CRM, constant innovation is needed because of rising customer expectations, increasing global competition, and better informed consumers.

All is flux, nothing stands still.

Heracleitus

CHAPTER 4

Technology

After reading this chapter you will be able to

- Appreciate the range of enabling computer and telecommunications technologies available for CRM

- Define common classifications of CRM software applications

- Understand the technological infrastructure requirements for supporting CRM

- Appreciate the issues involved in the integration of CRM technologies

- Appreciate the significance of technological trends on the future of CRM

As introduced in Chapter 1, CRM is a technology—specifically, a process—used to create consistent, repeatable, measurable results. Although technology is often associated with computers and electronics, most CRM is accomplished with manual processes that are based on multiline or switched telephone systems (see Figure 4-1). As shown in the figure, a typical process description for CRM in a company with a team of customer service representatives involves:

1. The customer contact, where the customer initially calls a customer service representative (rep)

2. The customer service rep verifies that the caller is actually a customer who is eligible for customer support. Callers may not be customers or may not be eligible for support because their free support period has expired or because they failed to register their product.

3. The customer service rep logs the call. The log serves as a basis for follow-up on the customer's problem as well as a data point for evaluating the effectiveness of the CRM effort.

4. The initial rep (rep A in the figure) triages the call to the rep (rep B in the figure) most qualified to handle the problem, based on the first rep's understanding of the problem and second rep's expertise or availability.

5. The second rep works with the customer to clearly define the problem.

6. The rep researches the problem.

7. The rep collaborates with other reps (rep C in the figure) in researching the problem and attempting to define a solution.

8. A rep documents the problem and the progress, whether the problem was fully addressed or left open. Open problems involve further research and contacting the customer when the problem is resolved.

9. The problem is closed when the solution has been identified.

10. The CRM department manager or administration uses the documentation of the problem and how it was handled in order to evaluate the effectiveness of the CRM effort.

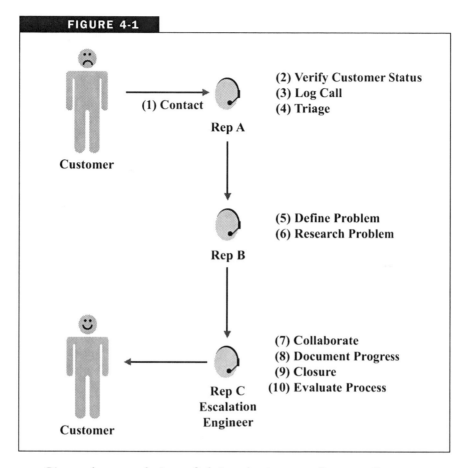

FIGURE 4-1

(1) Contact — Rep A

(2) Verify Customer Status
(3) Log Call
(4) Triage

(5) Define Problem
(6) Research Problem

Rep B

(7) Collaborate
(8) Document Progress
(9) Closure
(10) Evaluate Process

Rep C
Escalation
Engineer

Customer

Given the popularity of doing business online, or E-commerce (which accounted for about 1 percent of all retail activity in 2000), and the use of computers for cost savings, in most other areas of business, it is no surprise that CRM looks to computer technology for its promise of cost savings. Some of this computer technology resides in increasingly powerful telephone systems, and some in the connections between the telephone systems and PC networks, connected in a variety of configurations.

The goals in computerizing the CRM process are to protect the customer service rep from having to know its complexity and to improve the effectiveness of a CRM effort. As a result, a company should be better able to target services to specific customers, handle more customers in shorter time, save time for representatives and selected customers, and improve or at least hold the company's bottom line. Note that because of the increasing importance of CRM on E-commerce, eCRM is covered in depth in Chapter 5.

Most of the technologies discussed here apply to activities within a call center, traditionally referred to as a cost center because it represents a significant cost of doing business. In most organizations, a call center is a central place where service representatives, usually with some amount of computer automation, handle customer and other telephone calls. A call center might consist of one or two reps or hundreds of reps, depending on the support needed for a product or service, the amount of money allocated for customer support, and other business parameters. Before considering the technology options available for the modernization of a corporate CRM activity, consider how technology can affect CRM in a small business.

Pedaling Into the 21st Century

Going back to our three roommates, with all of the activity in her apartment surrounding bicycling, Debra can't help think about picking up a used bike for transportation to and from her classes. On Jen and Paul's recommendations, she stops by Hank's bike shop and finds a bike that is just right for her, but she doesn't have the money. While talking about payment plans with Hank, she notices one of the shop assistants going through Hank's file cabinet of customer profile index cards and suddenly has an idea. Debra can trade services with Hank and get the bike she wants. She offers to set up a computerized system to manage Hank's contacts and customers and provide a day of training in exchange for the bike. They discuss how the system could benefit Hank's business practice, both in the shop, with customers, and with vendors. They talk about the functions it would perform, as well as the cost of the technology Hank would have to buy—about $1,000 for the computer, $500 for a printer, $500 for a bar code reader, $200 for an uninterruptible power supply, and another $500 for the software. Finally, they discuss what Debra's compensation would be for setting up the system and for ongoing support. A day later, Hank calls Debra to tell her that it's a deal.

Debra orders a computer system, as well as the contact management and point-of-sale software from a well-established mail-order firm, using Hank's charge card. Hank wants the contact management computerized file to store the same information that his index cards do, so Debra configures the software to store customer name and address, each date of contact with the store, what was discussed, and any action Hank needs to take. The software also has an auto-dial feature that can automatically dial the phone number of a particular customer. The point-of-sale system allows sales to be automatically documented using a bar code reader tied to the cash register. Debra spends about two weeks writing a software interface that allows the point-of-sale system to automatically enter the sales information in the contact management database.

KEY TERM

Sales The process of selling or exchanging money for products and services.

After about one hour of training from Debra, Hank's first hurdle is entering the information from the card file into the computer's contact management system—a task he assigns to his assistants when they are otherwise idle. In keying in the data from the index cards, the assistants discover that Hank varied what he recorded over the years. When he first started the index card system, he was not as interested in the reasons customers bought bicycles, but focused on the sale itself, and sometimes Hank's shorthand was not decipherable, even to Hank. Some of the old data were therefore questionable. The next hurdle was training the assistants. Debra had to devote a few hours to teach the assistants to use the system, back up the data, and perform other routine maintenance.

Initially, Hank's reaction to the new system was mixed. He used the contact management software on a new sale and discovered that he forgot to specify a place to put in extra customer information, such as the customer's future bike-buying plans. As a result, he needed Debra to modify the system. He also had to make provisions for backups, power loss, viruses, and other causes of data loss. Hank also had a few privacy and security concerns. Whereas his index card system filled an entire filing cabinet, the entire customer contact database could fit on a floppy disk and be e-mailed to a competitor. On the positive side Hank realized that a fulfillment house could create an entire mailing without his intervention once it has a copy of the contact management database.

A few months into working with the system, Hank was pleased that he made the decision to computerize his sales and CRM activities. With a few keystrokes, he can sort customers by age, time since their last purchase, type of riding, and other variables that allow him to create personal letters to his best customers and general mailings to other customers. Hank is also acutely aware of the limitations of his small system. He spends more time entering data than he did before and feels both empowered by and dependent on the technology.

CRM Technologies: An Overview

As the story illustrates, computerizing a CRM activity means setting up processes that encompass several tasks. The first is deciding exactly which of the CRM processes should be computerized, from tracking the initial and subsequent sales to generating mailing lists of customers to receive notification of factory recalls or be notified of sales. Examples of CRM-related tasks and activities that are typically enhanced by computer technology are described in the following sections.

Analysis

The examination of customer information and call center activity for decision making, such as predicting customer behavior based on a specific level of customer support, is normally performed by call center managers and administrators. Typical analysis on internal CRM operations includes return on investment (ROI) for the CRM effort, customer service rep turnover, and projected workload. External or customer-focused analysis includes some measure of customer satisfaction.

Automatic Call Distribution

Automatic call distribution (ACD) is the automatic answering and routing of calls based on the characteristics of the call and the number of customers in each representative's queue. This function is key to the efficient operation of every call center. Routing can be based on a variety of factors, such as the customer problem or geographic origin of the call, based on caller ID information and data in the corporate database that links customer phone number with customer demographics and calling history. The idea is to keep customers on hold for the least amount of time, to minimize representative idle time, and to reduce the need to shift calls from one customer service representative to another.

Back-End Integration

The real-time, continuous communications of customer data from various touch points—including phone, mail, E-mail, wireless, and direct customer contact —among various computer systems, allows a seamless customer record to be created. In this context, the "back end" is normally associated with operations that involve hardware and software that reside in the corporate computer center, as opposed to "front-end" activities that occur on the representative's desktop PC.

Computer-Telephony Integration

Computer telephony integration (CTI) is the real-time integration of voice and computer data, allowing E-mail and phone data from the same customer to be routed to a particular representative. This feature is especially useful when representatives deal with customers who use E-mail and voice interchangeably, in that the integration provides continuity of services, regardless of the communications medium. CTI allows a customer to place an order through the Web and to later call a customer service rep to check the status of the order or modify the order before it leaves the company. Without CTI, reps either have to have two computers at their desks, one with a record of online transactions and one with a record of phone-in orders, or switch between two programs on their PC. In either case, the lack of integration results in an increased likelihood of errors, an inefficient use of rep time, and a longer wait for customers.

Data Aggregation

Aggregation is the process of moving data from a variety of sources into one location so that it can be rapidly accessed and analyzed.

KEY TERM

Telephony The transmission and reception of voice and data.

Data Collection

The process of capturing data from a variety of touch points, including telephone, E-mail, and direct customer contact, is the first step in data aggregation. As in the roommate story, data collection also includes inputting paper-based legacy data (Hank's card file), which often has to be manually keyed into a computer system.

Human Resources

Several human resources (HR) functions can benefit from computerization, including customer service representative scheduling, training, and qualifications for incentives; however, selecting customer service representatives takes a skilled HR professional who is able to identify potential effective employees. The ideal representatives have to be service-oriented, able to laugh at stressful situations, and work as a team. A good HR counselor can detect these qualities in an applicant.

Interactive Voice Response

Interactive voice response (IVR) is a telephone interface to a computer system driven by either voice responses or telephone keypad entries. IVR menu-driven responses replace human telephone operators, allowing customers to retrieve their bank account balances, request faxes of product information, or validate their credit card, for example, all automatically, without the aid of a person.

Localization

In the context of CRM, localization is the use of the appropriate language etiquette for customers, especially customers in other countries. Computers can help with localization by identifying the origin of callers and routing their calls to the customer service representative with the appropriate language skills. When applied to visual media, such as print publications and the Web, localization includes paying attention to the significance of certain colors and phrases. Some colors may offend or have a variety of meanings, depending on the culture. For example, red text is rarely used in Korea, especially in any form of personal correspondence. Similarly, some phrases may be too confusing when translated from English to the language of the customer.

Logging and Monitoring

Logging and monitoring includes the minute-by-minute recording of what each customer support representative is doing, allowing for evaluation of individual productivity, ROI, and other internal analyses. The recordings can be evaluated for training purposes to assess reps on their politeness, accuracy of information, and adherence to company policies. Monitoring is also used to settle disputes when a customer complains about customer service rep behavior.

Measurement

Computers can automate and simplify quantifying customer service performance. Examples of measurements that can be simplified through the use of computer technology include determining the length of the average time the customer service representative actually spends with a customer (handling time), the number of customer hang-ups while they're waiting to speak to a rep, the amount of time a customer waits in a telephone queue before speaking to a representative, and the time it takes for a representative to finish one call and move to the next one (turnover time).

Personalization

If the business can use customer-specific information to create a feeling of personal attention, then the customers may be loyal to the company or responsive to a target marketing campaign. For example, in the story, Hank may create two flyers, one for college students and one for customers who have children. Which catalog is sent to a particular customer depends on the customer's particular demographics.

KEY TERM

Marketing The process associated with promoting products or services for sale, traditionally involving product, price, place, and promotion.

Reporting

As in other areas of business, computers greatly simplify the task of generating reports from data stored in applications. Relevant reports include lists of customer complaints and customer service representative responsiveness, as measured by average speed of answer, average talk time, and some measure of the service level. Service level may be measured from the customer's perspective but is most commonly based on company-specified metrics.

Resolution

The methods by which customer problems are resolved can be greatly simplified by computer technology, especially when the problems are ongoing. When resolution isn't immediate, customer data and representative suggestions need to be tracked and made available to other customer service representatives in the call center.

Training

Customer service representatives tend to be the least trained of corporate employees, in part because of the expense and time involved; however, teaching customer service representatives how to use computerized CRM systems can be simplified through computer-based training (CBT). In addition, support personnel can use CBT to learn and review how to perform routine maintenance on the CRM hardware and software, including how and when to create data archives. Although good CBT can be expensive to develop in-house, the commercial packages are generally affordable enough to be used to supplement classroom training.

User Authentication

Computer-based tools are often indispensable in verifying that customer service representatives have access to the customer and corporate data they need to perform their jobs, but no more. The most common user authentication or security measure is a username and password combination.

Workforce Management

A variety of computer-based tools is available to help management allocate representative time effectively, reduce customer wait time, and forecast and schedule call center activity.

After deciding which tasks should be computerized, the next step in computerizing some aspect of the CRM operation is to decide on the software, hardware, and infrastructure requirements. In coming to this determination, there is always the issue of how to deal with legacy systems and data. The new computer system can either be integrated with or replace the legacy system. Another question is whether to integrate the CRM system with other systems used throughout the organization, such as point-of-sale, administrative, billing, and other systems in place or being planned. An integrated system where, for example, sales figures for telephone sales can go directly to a sales database, can have a huge positive impact on business processes ranging from accounting, flow of materials, and order fulfillment to just-in-time inventory.

In computerizing a CRM operation, there are also personnel issues to deal with, including training, who will be responsible for migrating legacy written or computerized data to the CRM system, and who will be responsible for ongoing maintenance.

Maintenance includes not only verifying that the printer cartridges, paper, and other disposables are replenished as needed, but also that the data are properly archived and that the system is protected against attack from hackers and viruses, as well as abuse by employees. In this latter area, password protection and other user authentication and security methods may be required to minimize the chances of tampering by employees, especially if the system is used to monitor employee productivity.

Finally, if the CRM load of the company is growing or more functions are desired, then scalability will eventually be an issue. Product selection will then be critical because some CRM systems are designed to work as stand-alone systems, whereas others can be networked and expanded to hundreds of stations. The challenge of scaling up to handle more customers is compounded if several centers across the United States or in other countries need to be connected, especially if there are language and cultural differences.

The technology-based products and services in the CRM industry are stratified into an array of vendor-created categories or spaces, many of which are often distinguishable only because vendors claim different market spaces. As shown in Figure 4-2, these various technologies can be lumped into one of four overlapping categories:

1. Computer software

2. Computer hardware

3. Processes and professional services

4. Telecommunications products and services

These four categories of technology typically have different relevance to a CRM project, depending on whether the CEO is interested in maintaining a CRM effort or starting a new CRM initiative. For example, a new CRM effort will rely heavily on products and services in all four categories. In contrast, a CEO interested in upgrading a

FIGURE 4.2

Computer Software

Analysis	E-commerce
Business Intelligence	E-mail
Call Center Management	Executive Decision Support
Campaign Management	Field Service
Channel Support	Help Desk Management
Communication Software	Information Protection
Computer-Based Training (CBT)	Marketing Automation
Contact Management	Middleware
Customer Loyalty Programs	Mobile Computing Solutions
Customer Service Automation	Operations
Data Aggregation	Security
Data Collection	Telemarketing
Data Mining	Territory Management
Data Warehousing	Voice Recognition
Database Management Systems	Workforce Management

Computer Hardware

Data Backup Systems	Peripherals
Monitors	Security Systems
Network Hardware	Uninterruptable Power Supplies
PCs	Wireless Devices

Process and Professional Services

Application Service Provider	Network Management
Back Office Integration	Online Resources
Call Center Services	Process Reengineering
Consulting	Software Design
Customer Communications	Staffing Services
Field Support Services	System Integration
Help Desk Support	Technical Outsourcing
Internet Support Services	Training/Education

Telecommunications

Call Center Equipment	Telephony Networks
Messaging	Wireless Systems
Paging Services	

company's CRM capabilities might consider investing in new telecommunications equipment, such as new, lightweight headsets for reps.

The following sections provide a discussion of the previously identified four categories of technologies. Each section highlights the most significant products and services within each category. Readers with particular needs can skip to the relevant sections, whereas those with minimal or nonexistent CRM capabilities can read each section sequentially.

Computer Software

Of the available CRM products, software is the most varied and variable in functionality and cost. As shown in Figure 4-2, software products range from communications support, computer-based training, and data warehousing to E-mail and voice recognition. Furthermore, many of the products classified under one of these categories often provide some degree of functionality in other areas as well. For example, a contact management program can be considered a data collection system, perhaps integrated with a voice recognition program to simplify data entry. (Voice recognition software, combined with the standard sound capture card in a PC, converts the spoken word into keystrokes, allowing the representative to enter data with minimum typing.) Many contact management programs add to the confusion caused by overlap in classification and functionality because they have an integrated or built-in E-mail system.

KEY TERM

Voice recognition The ability of a computer to recognize the spoken word for the purpose of data input and receiving commands (also called speech recognition).

The more important software applications from a CRM perspective include:

- Contract management
- Database management
- Data warehousing
- Data mining
- Decision support
- E-mail

Contact Management

As the story of the bike shop illustrates, contact management software is typically an all-in-one suite of integrated tools that supports CRM. A typical contact management software package includes a customer database, a method of recording the topic discussed with each call or E-mail—often with an automatic time and date stamp—a calendar with reminders, an integrated E-mail system, a phone dialer that dials the phone to automatically return a customer's call, and a variety of tools to create reports, including lists of customers who have unresolved problems. Contact management systems are typically available in inexpensive, stand-alone PC-based versions for small businesses and in enterprise versions that require major server hardware and that can support hundreds of customer service representatives.

Database Management

The software interface between the customer service representatives and the data stored in a computer system is a database management system (DBMS). The DBMS stores, processes, and manages data in a systematic, economic way. It simplifies and regulates the process of working with the records and files of a database by providing tools for ensuring security, querying relations among different data, removing duplicate data, and performing other housekeeping tasks. Because it provides access to customer, product, service, and employee data, a good DBMS is a prerequisite for any significant CRM effort.

FIGURE 4-3

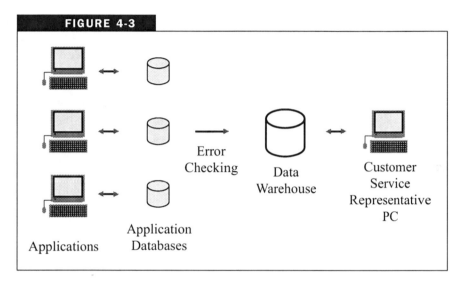

Applications   Application Databases   Error Checking   Data Warehouse   Customer Service Representative PC

Data Warehousing

A data warehouse is a central database, frequently very large, that can provide customer service representatives, call center managers, administrators, and other authorized users with access to a variety of information. A data warehouse, which is based on a DBMS, is different from a simple database in that it provides customer service representatives with data from a variety of otherwise noncompatible sources, such as a separate customer database, product database, order database, and inventory database.

Data warehousing software isn't a single program but is typically a suite of software tools that can be used to extract data from disparate databases, check for errors and duplicate data, and store the data in a data warehouse. As illustrated in Figure 4-3, a typical data warehouse incorporates data from several different applications into one accessible database. The data warehousing software links the hardware and various databases. The figure also illustrates that the software requires a significant hardware infrastructure.

Data Mining

Data mining software supports the process of extracting meaningful patterns from usually very large quantities of seemingly unrelated data. Data mining works by identifying relationships and correlations in data, such as the age range of customers who buy a particular toothbrush, the brand of toothpaste used by customers who spend more than $5 per year on dental floss, or the mean income of customers who buy first-class tickets for domestic travel.

The results of data mining are used in marketing, for example, to derive consumer preferences. Hank might discover, for example, that college students, who tend to be more active than older adults, tend to visit his shop more often than his older customers. Data mining is facilitated by access to large samples of customer data, such as is made possible by a data warehouse.

Decision Support

Decision support software comprises software tools that enable call center managers and company administrators to review and manipulate data in order to make better decisions. Decision support tools range from a simple spreadsheet program to a complex, graphical process simulator. They allow decision makers to visualize how changes in a current process can affect overall CRM throughput. With a process simulator, a manager could manipulate exactly how calls are distributed to customer service representatives and then view the effect of the change in the queue of customers on hold. A spreadsheet can be used to explore what-if analysis of various service scenarios, such as how adding one service representative would affect customer delay and the company's bottom line.

E-mail

Virtually every organization is linked internally, and often externally, with text-based E-mail. When it is used for customer contact, E-mail is normally integrated with a simple computer-based tracking system or a more powerful integrated voice and data system that tracks telephone and E-mail exchanges.

Although the software products are listed separately, they tend to be bundled with a variety of tools. For example, a contact management package might include an integrated E-mail system and word processor. Similarly, a decision support package might include a spreadsheet. When the CEO's task is to create CRM capabilities from scratch, this bundling can be a benefit because it ensures compatibility among tools. For example, in the story, Debra installed a contact management package for Hank that included a bundle of various tools that were guaranteed to be interoperable. When a company has already invested in an E-mail package, spreadsheet, and other software, however, the bundles can be an unnecessary expense. For a company interested in upgrading an existing CRM shop, purchasing a bundle to have access to one program can be expensive.

Computer Hardware

The continual upgrading of computer hardware is part of every modern CRM operation. This constant change is unavoidable, simply because what is considered a standard PC or server one month is obsolete and unavailable in six months. As a result, a company is likely to have several PCs and other computer hardware used in CRM, if only because some units eventually fail and have to be replaced by current technology. For the CEO establishing a new call center, the initial cost and performance figures will be critical; however, these decisions have to be made with the knowledge that computer hardware technology is evolving, often pulling companies along with it.

The computer software that provides the intelligence for supporting customer service representative activities is in turn built on top of a hardware infrastructure or platform that supports the software. Computer software and hardware are interdependent. Not only is either one useless by itself, but most systems also use some combination of software and hardware to get things done. For example, voice recognition software requires a microphone, a sound capture card in the PC, and the software. In addition, the performance and usability of the CRM system depends on how well the hardware and software work together. For example, a slow PC will render even the best software useless, and a fast PC will not make a poorly designed program any more usable.

Backup Hardware

Regularly archiving customer and company data, whether onto tape, CD-ROM, DVD, or other media, is a critical, inexpensive insurance against data loss or corruption. Stand-alone and networked CRM systems with only a few PCs may use inexpensive recordable CD-ROMs to archive data; however, for large call centers, server-based automatic tape backup hardware is used almost exclusively.

Monitors

When it comes to usability of computer hardware, the ergonomics of the monitor are particularly important. Flat, antiglare screens and high refresh rates can reduce eye fatigue and the headaches sometimes associated with staring at a computer monitor eight hours per day. Although most computers ship with inexpensive cathode ray tube (CRT) monitors, space limitations may dictate the use of more expensive, but often ergonomically superior liquid crystal display (LCD) monitors, which tend to be less susceptible to glare than CRT monitors.

KEY TERM

Ergonomics The system describing the physical relationship between the user and the computer and telecommunications hardware. The shape and layout of the keyboard, fit and weight of the telephone headset, room lighting, chair height and contour, desk and monitor height, monitor quality, and ambient lighting are all ergonomic factors that can enhance or decrease the effectiveness of a customer service representative.

Network Hardware

The lone PC, sitting on a desk without a printer or other peripherals, is virtually unheard of today. Virtually all modern PC installations use a network of some type to connect computers to printers, databases, and each other (see Figure 4-4). Networks can take on a variety of physical configurations, most of which use the Ethernet standard to communicate among devices. The most common elements of a computer network to plan for include:

- *Cables.* The physical cables that carry voice and data, from twisted pair and coaxial cable to fiber optics, are part of every wired network infrastructure. Because laying cables can be expensive, especially in older buildings, it's sometimes more cost effective to use a wireless network.

- *Firewall.* This is a device that blocks unauthorized users from accessing data on a corporate network. Hardware firewalls are more robust and pass authorized users more efficiently than software-based firewall programs that run on generic PCs.

FIGURE 4-4

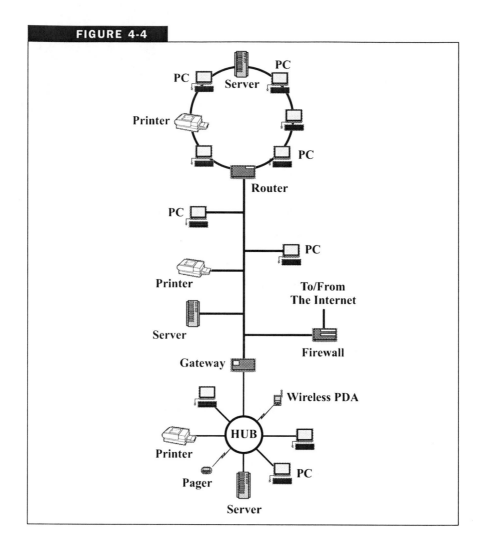

- *Gateway.* When there are multiple networks in an organization, and each uses different communications protocols, a gateway provides the translation so that data can flow freely from one network to the other.

- *Hub.* This is a device joining computers on a network at a single, central location. Small businesses—and homes—with more than one computer connected to the Internet use hubs to avoid paying for multiple connections to the Internet.

KEY TERMS

Ethernet A high-speed network standard that is often used to connect PCs, servers, printers, modems, and other peripherals.

Communications protocol A set of standards designed to allow computers to exchange data.

- *Modem.* This is used for dial-up connectivity to the Internet, through America Online or other internet service provider (ISP), especially from homes and small businesses. Although they are more universal, especially in small installations, most modems are limited to relatively slow 56K connections.

- *Network card.* This is an add-on card that adds Ethernet capabilities to a PC, allowing the PC to connect to the network.

- *Network printer.* A printer configured with an Ethernet port or connection so that it can be shared by multiple customer service representatives is one reason for having a network.

- *Router.* This is a device that forwards data to their correct destinations over the most efficient available route.

- *Server.* This is a computer that controls access to the network and Net-based resources. Although any PC can be used as a server, most are heavy-duty versions of a PC with relatively large amounts of RAM and hard disk space, and are designed to operate on a 24/7 basis. Servers are commonly used to store customer data as part of a data warehouse or contact management systems.

- *Wireless Devices.* Wireless personal digital assistants (PDAs) and pagers extend the network to mobile representatives and managers who may not be able to sit behind a desk all day.

Personal Computers

The personal computer (PC), the workhorse of the modern call center, is mostly a commodity item. From a CRM perspective, as long as a PC has sufficient RAM and hard disk space and a reasonably fast processor, the keyboard, mouse, and aforementioned monitor define its most important differences. An ergonomically correct keyboard and the use of a wrist support for the keyboard and mouse can help minimize the likelihood of a repetitive strain injury (RSI).

KEY TERM

Repetitive strain injury (RSI) A disorder of the tendons, ligaments, and nerves caused by repeated, prolonged repetitious movements, such as typing on a keyboard. The most common form of RSI in customer service representatives is carpal tunnel syndrome, which affects the wrists and hands and can result in the temporary total loss of functionality of the hands.

Security Systems

Customer data, like every other corporate asset, has to be protected from the curious, the disgruntled, and the mischievous. Although the ubiquitous username and password combination provides a good level of security against employees poking around data they have no business seeing, a variety of products are available for more serious threats, such as a computer-savvy hacker with malicious intent.

A popular way to keep prying eyes from specific data is to encrypt it such that only those with access to a decryption key can read the document. Whether encryption is based on special hardware or a software program, the basis of operation is the same, as shown in Figure 4-5. A simple but effective way to encrypt a text message is to shift each character by a certain number of places (the key in this example is "7") and

FIGURE 4-5

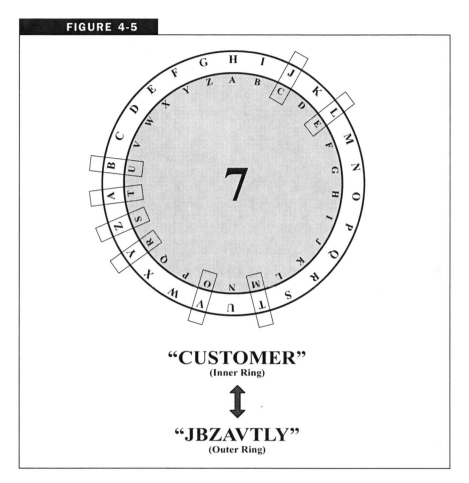

"CUSTOMER"
(Inner Ring)

↕

"JBZAVTLY"
(Outer Ring)

shift each character the opposite direction to decrypt it. Although this method is used by the secret decoder rings sometimes found in cereal boxes, the technique is often applied to highly sensitive computer data. In this example, "A" on the inner ring is shifted seven places to become "H," the eighth character of the alphabet on the outer ring. Note that case and numbers are not considered in the example, with the result that mapping repeats every 27 characters, given that there are 26 characters in the alphabet. When encryption is performed in hardware, more documents can be encrypted and decrypted per second than when software encryption and decryption is used.

Encryption The process of encoding data to prevent someone without the proper key from understanding the data, even though he or she may have access to the data. Because all encryption schemes can be broken with time, user authentication is considered more secure.

The other approach to security is to keep unauthorized users away from the data altogether, through a variety of user authentication schemes. One common security technology to authenticate users is the smart card. Smart card authentication systems are based on a 10- or 12-digit numeric code sequence that is generated on a credit card–sized device that serves as the representative's password. The sequence, which changes every minute, is unique to the smart card, which is registered to a particular representative. In addition, the call center computer system runs a program that generates the same password sequence and uses the sequence to verify the identity of the sender. Smart cards are more secure because they allow the customer service representative's password to change every minute or less, virtually eliminating the problem of someone guessing a representative's password, watching as the password is entered, or of someone using a "borrowed" password. The downside of smart cards is that they can be stolen or borrowed and returned without the owner's knowledge.

For advanced security, biometrics—the use of an individual's unique physical characteristics to verify identity—can be used. The most common biometrics measurements are fingerprint identification, hand geometry, voice verification, face recognition, iris scanning, and retina scanning. In each case, the user's image or sound is captured and analyzed, and a representation of it is stored in the computer system. In order to gain access to the computer system, the scan is repeated and

TIPS & TECHNIQUES

Uninterruptable Power

Some parts of the country are more often without AC power than others. California's rolling blackouts and the brownouts in the Northeast wreak havoc on computer-dependent customer support services. Precautions against power outages include:

- *Uninterruptable power supplies (UPSs) with the capacity to support the computer, monitor, and peripherals.* Small, personal UPS units about one-quarter the size of a typical PC are an inexpensive means of providing backup power for a half-hour or more for customer service centers with up to four or five representatives.

- *Diesel standby generators.* For larger call centers, diesel or other standby generators that automatically come online to power the entire customer service department for hours or days at a time are more economical than personal UPS systems. An added benefit of large generators is that power for lighting and air conditioning are powered as well—a necessity for 24/7 support.

- *Dual-grid AC supply.* In some areas, it's possible to simply switch from one power company to another in a matter of seconds.

- *Laptop computers.* For small support centers, battery-powered laptop computers have their own backup power.

- *Allowing or encouraging employees to work at home.* Distributing the workforce increases the odds that at least some employees will be available to field customer support calls or E-mail.

compared to the original. A close match authenticates the user. Voice verification has the advantage that sound capture hardware is built into most PCs, whereas hardware for capturing face, hand geometry, iris, or pupil images can be an expensive add-on.

Uninterruptible Power Supplies

Clean, reliable power for both computer and telecommunications equipment is a necessity for every CRM system, whether in a basement business or a 500-station call center. As the rolling power outages in California and across the United States in 2001 demonstrated, the high-tech industry quickly comes to a halt without power.

An uninterruptible power supply (UPS) not only removes the spikes and other sudden voltage variations from coming in from the power company, but it also has a battery-powered AC generator that takes over immediately in the event of a power disruption. The greater the capacity of the battery, the longer the computers attached to the UPS can operate without externally supplied AC power. Without a UPS, not only will computer and telecommunications equipment be inoperative during the outage, but the sudden interruptions in power can also permanently damage hard disks, monitors, and other computer equipment.

Processes and Professional Services

Many professional services are available to manage company resources, especially those related to CRM. The challenge specific to CRM initiatives is that most consultants and professional service companies that cater to the space have limited experience in CRM. As such, they are still learning how to implement CRM—at their customers' expense. That said, even a company with an experienced information services (IS) shop should consider outside services for new or ongoing CRM initiatives. Industrywide, only about one-quarter of IS projects in the

United States are completed on budget, on time, and to specifications. Given the expense of time overruns and failed projects, investing in a modest amount of outside consulting with a firm or individual with a proven track record in CRM can be a wise choice.

As shown in Figure 4-2, outside services range from application service providers (ASPs) and general consulting to process reengineering and training.

FIGURE 4-6

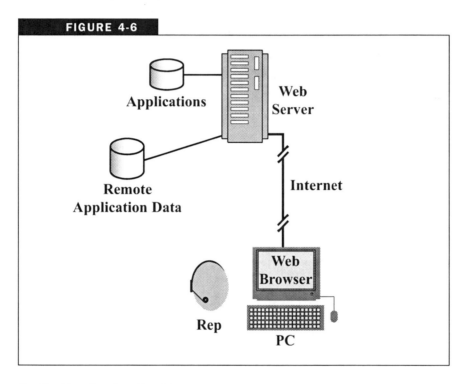

Application Service Providers

One of the most significant services is the ASP, illustrated in Figure 4-6. Unlike the traditional approach of purchasing software from a vendor and either loading it locally onto each PC or onto a corporate server, the ASP model offloads the software loading and maintenance task to an outside vendor. Customer service representatives use a standard Web browser to access a variety of software applications as though they were running locally; however, the cost savings of the ASP model can be significant because activities such as making data archives, loading new versions of software, maintaining a local server, and other IS functions are offloaded to the external vendor. As a result, the call center can operate with a much smaller technical support budget and staff than it could otherwise. The major downside to the ASP model is that if the vendor fails, customer data can become temporarily inaccessible. Therefore, it's important to select an ASP vendor who guarantees "up time" and stores customer data in escrow in the event that the vendor has financial difficulties and has to terminate operations.

System Integration

One of the most expensive and resource-intensive services that call centers typically rely on is system integration, in which different computer applications and systems are connected so they can share data. The goal of system integration is to allow representatives to access data they

---

IN THE REAL WORLD

The KISS (Keep It Simple, Stupid) Principle

Simply because the technology is available to trawl through multi-megabyte databases that are generated by customer interactions doesn't mean that other, less technically sophisticated approaches should be overlooked. For example, it rarely hurts to simply ask customers for information, as long as it's clear what the data will be used for. Companies like Reflect, the makeup and lifestyle product company, offer customers online questionnaires in exchange for a personalized Web site that features products most likely to appeal to the customer.

would otherwise have to look up manually or to give administrators in other departments access to CRM data in real time. For example, the contact management system might be integrated or interfaced with the accounting system so that representatives can verify that callers are actually customers and that they have bought technical support and their contract has not expired.

Because the applications in a typical corporation are often purchased from different vendors, sometimes years apart, and running on different hardware, system integration is usually a custom-programming task. As a result, system integration can take months of effort and considerable expense, with mixed results.

Telecommunications Products and Services

Long before computers entered the customer support scene, telephones and other telecommunications equipment were the basis for supporting customers remotely. Many small businesses rely solely on the telephone and—as in the story of the bike shop—a card file of customer data. Because virtually every business has a telephone system, the issue facing most CEOs is how to expand or enhance the existing telecommunications system. The modern call center relies on a range of telecommunications products and services, some of which are listed in Figure 4-2. The more significant telecommunications technologies, which apply equally to new CRM ventures and to existing call centers and small business support centers, are described in the following sections.

Call Center Equipment

In addition to a keyboard and monitor, customer service representatives interact with customers through telephones that are networked much like the computer system. Some networks share voice and data, whereas others are maintained separately (see Figure 4-7). Although the

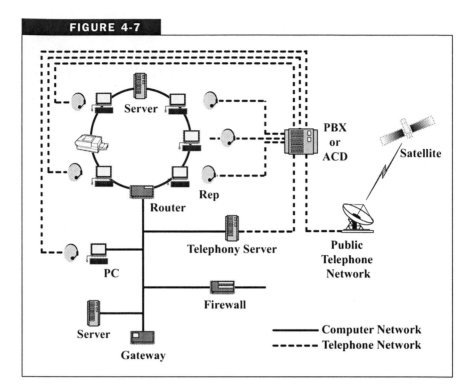

FIGURE 4-7

Server

PBX or ACD

Satellite

Rep

Router

Telephony Server

Public Telephone Network

PC

Firewall

Server

Gateway

——— Computer Network

- - - - Telephone Network

phone system and computer networks are shown as separate entities in the figure, some installations combine voice and data over the same network. This is accomplished through the use of middleware—software that translates the messages from the computer system to the phone system and vice versa. Regardless of how this infrastructure is configured, typical call center equipment includes:

- *Automatic call distributor (ACD).* This alternative to a private branch exchange (PBX) answers calls and puts them in specified order in a line of waiting calls. An ACD can be programmed, for example, to deliver calls to representatives in a predefined order or to representatives with the most idle time. Because of their sophistication, ACDs are usually more expensive than PBXs; however, despite their relative expense, ACDs are popular because they often provide greater value, in terms of functionality per dollar, compared to PBX systems.

- *Headset.* Hands-free telephone headsets are standard equipment in virtually every call center. The ergonomic and efficiency advantages of headsets over a standard telephone handset pay for themselves in reduced work-related injury claims and in the increased speed with which customer service representatives can handle calls. Depending on the physical setup of the customer service center, representatives may be much more effective using wireless headsets and telecommunications equipment.

- *Private branch exchange.* A PBX is a privately owned and operated central switching device. The PBX is what connects a call from a customer to a particular representative. It is much cheaper than having a separate phone line for each representative. A PBX supports modern, electronic telephones, with data displays, programmable buttons, call forwarding, and other features. An advantage of using a private switch instead of a public one is greater flexibility, cost savings, and the ability to select from a wider range of features and telephones.

- *Signboard.* This is a large data display, normally tied to the call center computer system, that lists call center activity statistics, as well as urgent messages. Statistics typically include the number of active, pending, and closed or resolved calls.

- *Telephone.* This is the desktop unit that supports voice-voice communications between customers and representatives. Most call center telephones are more complex than residential phones in that they may have an interface for a PC, special amplifier circuitry to support headsets, a light instead of an audible ringer, LCD screens, programmable keys, and other features that make their constant use more efficient.

- *Telephony server.* This is a computer that controls and manipulates phone, fax, and data. A telephony server can combine the functionality of several traditional devices, providing voice response, fax on demand, and conferencing.

Paging Services

Call centers are no different from other corporate divisions in their need for providing a means of rapidly contacting managers and staff regardless of their location. Paging services send messages to pagers, cell phones, personal digital assistants (PDAs), signboards, and E-mail addresses to ensure that prompt action is taken by the call center manager or representative. Paging services also ensure that vital messages get to field service reps and field trainers.

Wireless Systems

In many industries, customer support is no longer relegated to representatives who spend all of their working hours in a cubicle tethered to a wired telephone headset. In their role as customer support representative, an employee may need to visually inspect the progress of an order, walk to a different area in the department, or work with multiple computer systems. Similarly, a manager may need to be in constant telephone contact and yet be able to walk around dozens of cubicles to check on the progress of representatives. Wireless headsets, telephone systems, and PDAs provide freedom of movement without compromising connectivity. The main limitation of wireless systems is the added cost over wired systems and a modest increase in the security risk because wireless communications can be intercepted.

Technological Challenges

Although hundreds of companies serve the telecom and computer industries, the technologies available for CRM are far from stable. Numerous technological challenges need to be addressed before CRM software and hardware can be considered shrink-wrapped commodities. The more significant challenges include:

- Integration
- Scalability
- Achieving a positive ROI
- Ensuring that customers enjoy a reasonable level of privacy and security

These issues are relevant to every CRM initiative, regardless of scope or history.

Integration

Despite the advances made in the integration of voice and data and data from various computer applications and systems, integration is still an art in many instances. Although the telecom industry has standards for integration of voice signals, most computer systems use proprietary data formats. As such, the cost of integration can be significant, and the process may take days or even months, depending on the differences in the software involved. Integration is a multibillion-dollar industry.

Scalability

Unfortunately, an approach to handling CRM for a few customers at a time usually does not scale to handle dozens of simultaneous customer calls. Figure 4-8 illustrates how every computer and telecommunications system is designed with a particular load in mind, and exceeding that load can cause the system to fail. A server may run out of disk space; there may not be enough memory in the server to handle the load; and the telecommunications PBX or ADC may not be able to handle the number of phones needed.

The major practical issue associated with scalability is cost. Up to a point, the marginal cost or system delay associated with handling an additional customer is small. After that point, however, each customer that must be handled can cost considerably more than the previous one,

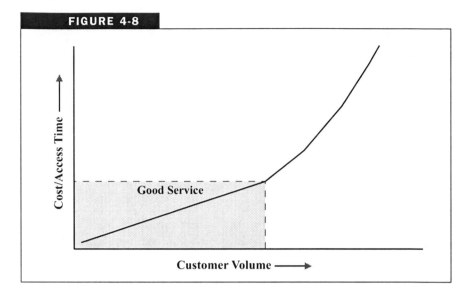

FIGURE 4-8

in terms of how much overall system performance is decreased. In the figure, note that there is initially a linear relationship between the number of customers handled by the system and the cost or access time, where access time is equivalent to the time customers spend on hold before their call is answered.

Positive Return on Investment

CRM, and CRM technology specifically, costs money. As noted earlier, call centers are traditionally referred to as cost centers, in part because customer support is often viewed as a cost of doing business. Even so, it is possible for technologies to either decrease this cost or to create greater customer and company value while maintaining a constant cost. In other words, the challenge is realizing a positive ROI. In this regard, the main choice is deciding between investing in computers and telecom infrastructure, training, and other HR issues or using offshore labor. In most cases, domestic call centers cannot compete on a cost basis with the service provided by centers operating out of India and other developing countries where labor is inexpensive.

Security and Privacy

Security and privacy are complex issues that involve technology, public policy, and common sense. In the CRM world, security normally refers to the ability to keep hackers and disgruntled employees from accessing and destroying customer and company data. Privacy is more about keeping certain data away from prying eyes, especially data that customer service representatives don't need in their work. As noted earlier, advances in security have been made in the use of biometrics, such as fingerprint recognition, and in the development of firewalls and other hardware that regulates access to sensitive data; however, every security system known can be defeated, given enough time.

Privacy is often more of a policy issue than a technical limitation, in that customers often expect the information they share with customer service representatives to stay within the company and not be sold to other companies. Many online companies, for example, lost business when customers discovered that their demographic information had been sold to other online companies and telemarketing firms for a profit.

CRM Focus

For the sake of clarity, most of this chapter focuses on the call center component of CRM; however, when properly implemented, CRM extends beyond mere call center activity. Sales and marketing have a stake in CRM because it can lead to increased sales revenue from existing and new customers. This sales activity can result directly from buyers evaluating the value of a product or service, based on the customer service record of the company. For example, Dell's main selling point isn't low prices—dozens of PC manufacturers vie for that position in the marketplace. Dell is one of the most popular computer companies because of its renowned customer service.

Although marketing and sales are separate and distinct activities, each can use CRM and call centers. For sales, call centers represent a source of qualified leads. Customer contact information, from E-mail addresses and cell phone numbers, provide sales professionals with pre-qualified sales lists. For example, a customer who has already purchased a product from the company may be interested in a new model, an upgrade, routine maintenance, or an add-on product or service.

From a marketing perspective, CRM represents a vast source of customer feedback that can be used to tailor the marketing message to fit actual customer profiles. For example, if most customers calling in for support for a given product are younger than 25 years old, then the marketing campaign can be adjusted to appeal more to that age group. Alternately, if the product is designed for all age groups, then marketing could create a new program that appeals to customers of all ages. From a product design and engineering perspective, CRM and call centers represent a pipeline to paying beta testers—customers who unwittingly help debug a product or service they have paid for. Outright product failures, poorly written directions, and failure when products or services are applied to situations not initially planned for are all important data for engineering staff to work from. For example, if Hank's customers routinely complain that their bike chains rust quickly after they ride in the rain, he may switch to a new chain lubricant.

Customers who complain of service-related disappointments are key to improving that service. The best design changes often come from those customers who cause customer service reps the most trouble because they complain vehemently about their problems. Although it may be difficult for the customer reps to appreciate this situation at the time, customers who never call with complaints but rather simply turn to a competing brand of product or service represent not only lost future revenue, but valuable data as well.

Future Trends

Given the trend toward pervasive computing—the anytime, anyplace access to computer technology and data—it's likely that CRM will evolve in the next few years to be more responsive to customer needs. For example, with telematics, the use of mobile computing and telecommunications technologies to get directions, choose the best route, find the closest bank, and automatically call a service center in the event of an automobile accident, immediate customer feedback is mandatory.

KEY TERM

Telematics Mobile computing and telecommunications.

The combination of global positioning systems (GPS), wireless communications, and computer technology is only beneficial when response is immediate, such as when a business traveler is lost and in need of directions. This need for responsiveness places a greater demand on customer support because many users will not tolerate waiting on hold and listening to elevator music five minutes before a major meeting; however, there are instances where telematics can operate in a background mode, such as periodically transmitting diagnostic data to automobile dealers who can schedule maintenance as needed

Most of the future trends in CRM technologies, such as the use of virtual customer service representatives, where computers engage customers in E-mail dialogues, are linked to advances in the Web. Therefore, Chapter 5 continues with a look at technology and CRM, from the perspective of the Web and E-commerce.

Summary

One of the greatest challenges is integrating the various CRM technologies into one cohesive unit. To this end, the emergence of pervasive computing, where computer technology becomes woven into the fabric of everyday life, potentially offers anytime, anywhere customer support possibilities. The range of CRM computer and telecommunications technologies that every CEO should at least be familiar with include computer software and hardware, process and professional services, and telecommunications equipment and services. CRM software applications include analysis, computer-based training, data mining, data warehousing, database management, E-mail, and security. Infrastructure technologies include not only computer hardware, including networks, wireless devices, and data backup systems, but also telecommunications systems, including voice switching, voice network, and a variety of call center equipment. Only by knowing what types of technologies are available can a CEO be competent in directing the development of a new CRM effort or maintaining an existing one.

The better telescopes become, the more stars there will be.

Gustave Flaubert

eCRM

After reading this chapter you will be able to

- Understand the concept eCRM
- Appreciate what eCRM can deliver today and what customers want it to deliver
- Define the range of evolving technologies that can be applied to eCRM
- Understand the inevitable folding of eCRM into traditional CRM

In simplest terms, eCRM is customer relationship management on the Web; however, eCRM also includes the use of E-mail, E-commerce activity, and any other Internet-based customer touch points. The Web is an increasingly important touch point from the perspective of CRM, even though it accounts for much lower sales or customer support volume compared to the telephone, which is today's predominant CRM touch point.

E-Commerce The sale of goods and services over the Web.

The volatility of the E-commerce space, given the dotCom crash of 2000, has raised privacy issues and concern with security risks because of the uncertainty regarding the future of many dotComs. For example, customers are increasingly averse to giving personal information to an online store. Customers are also increasingly aware that when E-commerce companies are acquired, their mailing lists and other customer data are treated like any other business asset—they are sold to other companies for profit. Also, online customers are keenly aware of the increased security risks associated with business transactions on the Web.

The Web, however, is still in the public eye. Although Web-based sales account for only about 1 percent of total retail sales in the United States, there are significant markets where E-commerce is considerable and growing. Airline ticket sales over the Web are a little less than 10 percent industrywide, with some airlines realizing more than one-quarter of their ticket sales through self-service Web portals.

Customers have come to expect greater value for their money in Web-based transactions compared to other touch points. In some cases expectations are so high that customers expect value for little or no money—a holdover from early dotCom days when many companies literally paid customers to visit their Web sites. This entitlement attitude is changing with the realization that the dotComs that gave value away did not survive.

Despite a volatile background, the Web has a lot going for it. Unlike other touch points, the Web is superbly suited to gathering data directly from customers and automatically storing it in a database that can be searched and analyzed. In addition, because of the continued activity of companies developing software applications for the Web, an increasing number of CRM products enter the market every few weeks.

Although it is often difficult to keep up with the pace of creativity and change in the Web space, the Web is successful in extending the reach of CRM to anyone connected to the Web through dial-up modem, high-speed direct connection, or wireless modem. Companies are increasingly posting lists of frequently asked questions (FAQs) and their respective answers on the Web to lighten call center traffic. Similarly, many industries are focusing on the Web as a means of delivering services that are linked to CRM. For example, the major airlines and most travel agencies generate Web-based itineraries, including local weather, car rental rates and availability, and other travel-related information. For business travelers, the Web represents an omnipresent reference to flight data, hotel information, weather, and travel help in general.

As noted in Chapter 4, the increasing relevance of wireless Web devices in business and the rise in pervasive computing in all levels of society suggests that eCRM will become increasingly important. In addition, evolving technologies have the potential to transform traditional CRM as well. The following section is a continuation of the story of Hank's bike shop that leads to a more in-depth discussion of eCRM.

 Web Presence

It has been several months since Debra installed a computer-based CRM system in Hank's bike shop. In that time, Hank and his assistants totally replaced the paper-based system that Hank maintained for decades with a contact management software package. Now Hank and his assistants record all day-to-day activity on the computer system. He has not completely given up paper, however; at the end of every month, he prints everything out, puts the printouts in a three-ring binder, and brings it home for safekeeping. He knows that computer technology, no matter how advanced, is not immune to catastrophic failures and data loss.

Although Hank is generally happy with his system, he has noticed that the big bike shop across town has a Web site, and he thinks he should have one as well. He calls Debra and discusses what would be involved in setting up a Web site for his bike shop. After a few minutes of negotiation, they decide on a new barter arrangement, and Hank's bike shop has a Web site up within a few weeks.

The Web site lists his store hours, directions to his shop, maps of local bike trails, tips on bike care, and a list of specials to new and existing customers. Hank works with his assistants to come up with a list of the most frequently asked questions that cause their customers grief. Hank compiles the list, answers all of the questions, and has Debra post the list on the Web. As a result, the number of calls to Hank that deal with mundane warranty issues drops dramatically. Overall, business is up as well, especially since some of the specials listed on the Web site are targeted at students of the nearby campus where Debra attends class.

Hank is pleased with his Web presence, especially since Debra's work is clearly superior to what the competing bike shop has on the Web; however, he finds that he is spending more time on the Web site and the contact management system than he likes. He isn't sure of the return on investment for the time he spends answering E-mail, adding to the list of FAQs, gathering information on local biking events, and generating postcards and E-mail to remind customers to visit the shop. Hank is concerned that when he or his assistants are spending time gathering information for the Web site, they are spending less time with customers, taking care of inventory, or repairing bikes. Despite his doubts, through casual conversation with his customers, Hank learns that most customers appreciate the three-month E-mail reminders they receive from him to come in for their free tuneup after purchasing a new bike. More often than not, when customers return to pick up their newly serviced bike, they also buy a bike pump, riding glasses, or some other accessory.

In one of their regular monthly meetings to check on the status of Hank's computer system, Debra tells Hank about a project in one of her computer science classes. She is using ChatterBots—software robots— to carry on real-time conversations with Web users. The technology has evolved to the point that many users do not even know that a computer, not a human, generates the responses to their queries. Debra offers to put the technology on Hank's Web site at no charge, as long as she can use the data for her course. Hank agrees, and Debra goes to work.

KEY TERM

Bot A software robot that can be programmed to perform a variety of tasks, from locating a Web page containing a particular word or phrase, to replying to text statements and questions in real time.

Debra sets up a ChatterBot on Hank's Web site, using the list of FAQs that Hank previously compiled, which enables the Bot to answer questions posed to it in E-mail. For example, when a customer sends Hank a message:

"How long does it take for an overhaul and how much does it cost?"

The ChatterBot automatically replies:

"It generally takes about a week for a complete overhaul, which includes new cables, a chain, and brake pads. The cost is $95. If you are a student or if you bought the bike here, the cost is $80. All work is guaranteed for 30 days. If you're not satisfied with the work during that time, bring the bike back in and we'll make it right."

To Hank and Debra's delight, customers apparently cannot tell the difference between Hank and the ChatterBot. As a result, Hank can focus on the operation of his bike shop and leave the ChatterBot to handle most E-mail questions. Customers still think that Hank takes time out of his busy day to answer their E-mail messages. Although Hank realizes that the Web is just one of the touch points he relies on for his business, he is genuinely pleased with what Debra managed to accomplish in only six months. It is clear that although the current state of affairs is not perfect, the technology is rapidly evolving to the point that not having a modern CRM system or a Web site is a business liability.

TIPS & TECHNIQUES

Value of the Web

The value of the Web as a touch point for product information and support depends on customer demographics, the type of product that must be supported, and the other touch points available to customers. For example, a Web touch point is most valuable when the following conditions exist:

- Customers are computer literate and likely to be online at least one day a week.

- The Web can provide more and better information than is available through other means, such as print media. For example, many highly technical products lend themselves to animation and other graphical treatments.

- The marginal cost of publishing information for a particular product is lower on the Web than through other means.

- Product variability—in price, specifications, or configuration —is high. Because the price of updating information on the Web is typically much lower than printing, for example, it's optimum for keeping customers up to date on bug fixes, FAQs, and other news.

- The volume of traffic on the Web site is high. Companies that provide outstanding support through their Web site benefit from lower call and E-mail volumes.

Web and eCRM

Most people consider the Web, like the fax and telephone, to be part of everyday business. Except for perhaps the corner food store, virtually every business has a Web presence. It is simply expected; however, this expectation is a constantly evolving one. Whereas a simple marketing banner was acceptable only a few years ago, today customers expect more in a Web site. A simple electronic billboard that lists a company's name and address may even be considered a turnoff, depending on the customer. Today, interactivity and functionality are key to the success of any Web site, and part of this interactivity is expected to include eCRM.

Fortunately, the Web is ideally suited to providing eCRM. Some of the characteristics of the Web as a touch point for eCRM are listed in Figure 5-1 and described in the following sections.

Affordability

Although a major Web presence can cost millions of dollars, basic CRM functionality, such as lists of FAQs, links to E-mail and related sites, and hosting ongoing discussion groups can be developed and maintained

---

FIGURE 5-1

Advantages of the Web in eCRM

Affordability	Immediacy
Amenability to new technology treatments	Low marginal cost
	New CRM service opportunities
Availability	Omnipresence
Degree of integration	Personalization
Enhanced customer data collection	Popularity
	Repurposable content
Enhanced interactivity	Self-documentation
Flexibility	User control
High information density	Fun factor

---

for less than the cost of a customer service representative. This is possible because Internet service providers (ISPs) are now commodity items. The tools available for Web design are mature enough to be used by virtually anyone. Most of the cost is usually associated with creating content for a Web site. For example, in the story, Hank had to take time to develop a list of FAQs and answer them.

The more involved technologies that may be associated with a Web presence, such as data warehousing and data mining, may involve significant hardware, software, and personnel costs. The cost issues associated with CRM are discussed in more detail in Chapter 7, "Economics of CRM."

Amenability to New Technology Treatments

A variety of evolving Web-based technologies can be applied to eCRM. For example, customer profiling, virtual customer service representatives, and other software tools can be used to address eCRM goals. Because vast amounts of customer data can be gathered from the Web, technologies such as data warehousing and other data-intensive applications may have even more applicability on the Web, compared to data from other touch points. Furthermore, because the Web can be highly interactive, new approaches to CRM can be applied in ways not possible through any other touch point.

Availability

The Web is available to most customers on a 24/7 basis. Although automated telephone support, printed materials, and fax on demand may be accessible at any time as well, the Web differs in the type of information that can be accessed on a continual basis. That is, like telephone support—which is rarely available all day, every day—the Web can be interactive, delivering exactly what the customer is looking for with a minimum of waiting or the need for other equipment, such as a fax machine.

Degree of Integration

The Web can be integrated with business processes to a degree only approachable by other touch points. Amazon.com and Federal Express illustrate how the Web allows customers to freely access data related to their shipments. Although the same information could be delivered by telephone, either through an automated system or a customer service representative, the Web is more efficient and, in most instances, much faster. Another aspect of integration is the benefit of being able to print out, for example, package tracking information, preventing at least one kind of error in tracking the delivery of a product—incorrectly writing down the information given by a representative or an automated phone system.

A company with a fully integrated Web site—one that shares data with phone, fax, and retail outlets, for example—can offer a variety of evolving customer support services. One service that relies on full touch point integration is preemptive eCRM, in which interactive, machine-generated alerts are automatically generated to remind or notify customers of events. For example, Orbitz, the large online travel site backed by the major airlines, uses preemptive eCRM to notify customers by E-mail, pager, or phone when flights are canceled or delayed. Similarly, alerts can be generated to remind customers that it is time to download the latest virus definitions for an antiviral utility or bring their car back to have the oil changed. Once contacted, customers can choose to connect to a customer service representative, salesperson, or simply acknowledge receipt of the message. An advantage of using interactive alerts, which rely on touch point integration, is that companies can employ a smaller call center staff.

Enhanced Customer Data Collection

Customers can be tracked in their use of a Web site, providing the company with data on the information customers seek and, by extension, value most. Similarly, if customers transact business through a Web site, then demographic and other customer information are immediately available for marketing and other purposes. In contrast, many customers may navigate through an interactive voice response system on a telephone, leaving the company with no specific data about customer preferences.

Enhanced Interactivity

A Web site designed for CRM can provide enhanced interactivity. For example, instead of being put on hold to listen to music for 10 minutes at a time, customers can exchange E-mail with a live customer representative or from computer programs that simulate representatives, which can respond immediately to customer questions. Although most of these programs are no match for a live representative, the interactivity possible on the Web is generally superior to that of other touch points.

Flexibility

The Web is a highly flexible medium. Given the wide variety of affordable Web development software tools available, it is possible to modify a Web site, including content focused at particular customers, to fit the changing needs of customers or to accommodate new products. Because most changes to a Web page are cheap to make, and do not incur the major cost that changes to print materials do, modifications and improvements can be ongoing.

High Information Density

The Web provides a high density of information, in part because of the multimedia capabilities of the medium. Sounds, text, graphics, pictures, animations, and video can be used to present information to customers in a way that a telephone conversation between a customer and a customer sales representative cannot. A single Web page can present a video to illustrate the proper operation of a product, a list of FAQs and answers, and a textual description of other remedies, including how to contact customer support and other company contact information. With a good Web page design, a customer can see at a glance the available features or categories of information and immediately locate content of interest.

Immediacy

In a culture where immediate gratification is the norm, the immediacy of the Web is a welcome attribute. An increasing proportion of customers in the United States have Web access at work and dial-up access from home. As such, accessing a Web site for customer support is usually only a few mouse clicks and a few seconds away. Immediacy is aided by many tools available, including powerful search engines that allow rapid, intuitive navigation through the information-rich Web space.

Low Marginal Cost

Once a Web site is constructed, the cost of adding an additional Web customer is typically very low. Unlike sending flyers and newsletters, which must be printed and mailed, adding an additional online customer at worst results in a negligible degradation in performance of the overall Web site. At some point, the added overhead of hundreds of customers will require a larger, more powerful server; however, if an external ISP hosts the Web site, then the ISP assumes responsibility for accommodating the additional customer Web traffic.

New CRM Service Opportunities

Because of the extent to which the Web is technologically based, new CRM service options can be tried in a variety of scenarios. For example, real-time E-mail can be integrated with a Web site to provide a more seamless customer service experience, and retail outlets can accept return items ordered on the Web. For example, as a result of the integration of customer information from eCRM, GAP Inc. allows customers to purchase items on the Web and return them to retail outlets, without the hassle of packing up the item and then standing in line at the post office to mail the package.

As an example of a new CRM service opportunity, consider that the Web can be linked to live telephone support, providing live, one-on-one support for online shoppers. The mail-order and online clothes retailer Lands' End offers this service, which allows customers to browse their online store with the assistance of a customer service representative. As a result, fewer customers abandon their carts before they check out of the Lands' End online store.

In addition, as outlined in the story, ChatterBots and other forms of Bots can be used to automatically respond to customer queries. Although the technology is still evolving, Bots can help customers solve problems on a 24/7 basis, usually without the intervention of live representatives.

IN THE REAL WORLD

Playing the Fans

The National Basketball Association (NBA) is engaged in a CRM initiative with a goal of providing insight into basketball fans. Scoring in this arena involves using a CRM system to create personalized promotions in Europe, Asia, and Australia. Instead of simply creating generic brochures that are distributed to all three markets, the NBA highlights teams and players that are popular with fans in each market, increasing the odds that fans will attend local games.

Omnipresence

The wireless Web, and other innovations that make the Web pervasive in our everyday lives, enhance the value of the Web as a touch point for eCRM. Some new cars come equipped with Web-based direction finders, programs that pinpoint the location of the nearest ATM or restaurant, or technologies that automatically notify emergency services. BMW Assist, Mercedes-Benz's Tele Aid, General Motor's OnStar, and Ford/Qualcomm's Wingcast use the Web to deliver information and services to their mobile customers. When lightweight wireless personal digital assistants (PDAs) become as popular as cell phones—or when more cell phones provide moderate to high-speed access to the Web—it will be even harder to escape the Internet's omnipresence.

Personalization

Information on Web sites can be personalized to fit the specific needs of particular customers. Technologies such as cookies—files that allow Web sites to recognize returning visitors—support personalization to almost any degree. Cookies allow Amazon.com's Web site to greet customers by name, provide information on books and DVDs most likely to be of interest to customers, and remember information, such as mailing address, charge card number, and previous orders. Although some customers set their browsers to refuse cookies for privacy reasons, personalized interaction saves customers time, allows them to avoid the hassle of having to remember passwords and long strings of credit card numbers, and increases the likelihood that they will return.

Popularity

Many customers first look to the Web for information, saving needless calls to customer support representatives. As more and more companies post information online and the likelihood that information will exist

KEY TERM

Cookie A file written to a customer's hard drive by a Web server that identifies the customer on subsequent visits to the site.

online increases, use of the Web to look up information will become more popular.

Repurposable Content

Content developed for the Web can be used in print publications, to drive voice interfaces, and for other touch points. For example, in the story, Hank can print out maps of bike trails from his Web site and make them available to walk-in customers.

Self-Documentation

When used with E-mail, the Web is a self-documenting touch point. The customer and, to a much lesser extent, the customer service representative are intimately involved in creating documentation of their problems and questions about a product or service. In other words, most of the labor involved in documenting complaints is passed on to the customer. The effect of this added burden can be minimal or, if the customer is already at wits end about a problem, he or she may balk at the prospect of losing yet more time.

User Control

Customers can be given the ability to self-direct their search for information. In effect, the Web becomes a self-service CRM station. Federal Express and Amazon.com offload the common customer service representative task of locating a package or shipment by giving customers access to tracking data. As a result, customers are in control, and customer sales representatives are available to handle other tasks. Ideally, the information is provided in a nonlinear fashion that allows customers to access information directly, without having to be exposed to unwanted material and information, as is the case with interactive voice response (IVR).

Fun Factor

A properly constructed Web site—one with animations, graphics, sounds, and simulations—can be fun, especially when the alternative is waiting on hold on a telephone for a customer service representative. In this regard, the Web can be considered a form of edutainment—a place where customers gain supporting data while in an entertaining environment.

The evolving Web is far from perfect, and it should not be considered a replacement for the telephone, E-mail, and other CRM touch points. Some customers expect nothing less than a personal telephone call from a customer service rep, whereas others are content with an E-mail acknowledgement. When the Web is integrated with other touch points, however, it can improve the overall CRM experience and increase the company's bottom line.

E-Customer Expectations

Many of the characteristics of the Web that make it ideally suited for eCRM are self-limiting. For example, immediacy not only means that customers can access information about a particular company within a few mouse clicks, but customers can go to the competition as well. This possibility is increasingly relevant, given that the hype surrounding the Web has increased customer expectations to the point that a less than perfect experience is not tolerated.

Recall from Chapter 2 that the parameters associated with a positive Loyalty Effect are value, investment, difficulty locating alternatives, and a positive emotional bond, while the factors associated with a negative Loyalty Effect are the number of affordable alternatives and customer frustration. Therefore, it is obvious why customer loyalty is an issue on the Web. Customers often need a compelling reason to frequent a particular Web site, given that alternatives abound and tolerance for frustration is low. Customers expect a good deal, and they expect it immediately.

Despite the downturn in the economy in 2000 and 2001, and the demise of many dotCom ventures, customers generally expect to save money on the Web. Although some Web sites clearly offer different reasons for shopping (e.g., Amazon.com promotes its personal service, not its prices), some companies are profiting from the lowest-price mentality. Examples of companies in this class of application are Gator.com and Dash.com. The programs from these companies virtually steal customers away from online stores by preempting transactions with a particular vendor and offering the same product at a discount through another online vendor. Gator.com is a free portal that users can use to access any Web site. Dash, in contrast, is a free, downloadable program that a user can elect to run locally when surfing the Web.

When the customer places an order for a particular item, the Gator.com Web portal checks affiliated vendors for prices on the same item and offers the customer the discount if they go through their affiliated vendor, by merely clicking on a link. Dash works similarly, but unlike Gator.com, it alerts the customer to better prices by posting a message on a bar that sits on the bottom of the screen of the Web browser. Both programs learn where customers shop and become virtual shopping partners. Because the vendor pays, the customer has little to lose by using either program. To alleviate customer resistance to using the service because of privacy concerns, these programs do not store the customer's demographics or the sites visited, but the data remain on the customer's PC.

Given customer expectations, any company that does business on the Web has to provide excellent customer service. In many cases, the level of service should be higher on the Web than it is for standard retail operations, at least in terms of speed of response. Customer support is increasingly considered part of a product or service. In this paradigm, getting a package to a customer via overnight mail does not constitute full delivery. If it takes a week to get a decent response from a customer service representative so that the product can be put to use, then delivery time is virtually a week, and the customer will likely never return to the company to do more business.

Fortunately, companies involved in E-commerce have an increasingly broad selection of eCRM computer technologies to help satisfy their low-tolerance, high-expectation E-customers. Some of the more promising eCRM technologies are described in the next section.

eCRM Computer Technologies

The computer technologies introduced in Chapter 4, including data warehousing, customer profiling, and decision support, are all applicable to eCRM; however, the Web and related computer developments make a variety of additional technologies that can be applied to eCRM. The common denominator in most of these technologies is the Web, or some other means of accessing the programs with standard hardware and software. Most often, no special applications need to be installed on the customer's PC; only a standard Web browser is required. In other words, they follow the ASP model defined in Chapter 4. The more notable technologies, discussed in the following section, include:

- Voice portals
- Web phones
- Bots
- Virtual customer service representatives

119

Voice Portals

Voice portals allow users to access the content on a Web site through a cell phone. This is possible with technologies such as VoiceXML (voice extensible markup language). Web sites written with VoiceXML (in addition to standard HTML, or hypertext markup language) can provide Web access with a standard wired or cellular telephone.

Commercial voice portals, such as BeVocal, TellMe, and Shoptalk, provide voice access to stock quotes, movie listings, and daily news. Other portals provide information on hotels, car rental agencies, and airlines and allow customers to make or confirm reservations, buy tickets, determine rates, obtain driving directions, verify store hours, and claim their frequent flyer miles. In this way, automatic services can reduce call center costs, especially for package tracking, account status, and answering FAQs.

The current limitation of voice portals on the Web is that the voice recognition is limited to particular domains, and each domain requires a different grammar. Building the grammar is time and resource intensive. For example, a voice portal that understands questions related to airline reservations can't be used in a stock market trading application. Instead, a grammar is needed that corresponds to words and phrases typically used in stock trading. In other words, the state of the technology is such that it works with good accuracy in a limited, well-defined area, with a vocabulary of perhaps several hundred words.

Web Phones

Otherwise known as Internet protocol or IP telephony, Web phone technology supports voice communications over the Internet, obviating the need for the telephone network. In theory, this allows a fuller integration of voice and textual data. Customer service reps need only a standard Web browser and a PC with a standard sound card to use IP telephony. The current constraint is in the supporting network infra-structure that replaces the switching functions of the PBX described in Chapter 4. Several companies, including 3Com, Cisco, and Mitel, are experimenting with IP telephony systems that can be applied to CRM.

Bots

Software robots or Bots are common on the Web. As shown in Figure 5-2, they're used to locate Web sites, as intelligent agents that use plain English (natural language search) to locate content on the Web, and as conversational engines that work in real time (ChatterBots) or through E-mail messages (E-mail Bots).

FIGURE 5-2

Bot Classifications	Examples
Search Engines	Yahoo, WebCrawler
Natural Language Search	Ask Jeeves, Brightware, InterMedia
ChatterBots	Artificial Life, NativeMinds
E-mail Bots	EGain, Kana Communications

With the exception of standard search engines, these Bots all make use of natural language processing (NLP), which allows a user to converse in natural English sentences instead of using keywords. For example, the ChatterBot in the bike shop story is able to recognize certain words and phrases in the customer's question and respond appropriately. No real intelligence or understanding is involved. NLP is simply a pattern-matching technology. When presented with a particular pattern—or one close to a particular pattern—it sends a predefined message to the customer or user. The time-intensive component of working with Bots for a particular CRM application is specifying the possible questions that customers might ask and providing a reasonable response for each query.

An advantage of using a Bot over a live customer rep is that responses are consistent. Unlike a customer rep, who may be having a bad day or is new on the job, the answers that Bots give to certain questions are always the same, unless the Bot is programmed otherwise. Another advantage is that Bots, unlike customer reps, scale (i.e., a Bot can handle one or one hundred simultaneous customers, even with modest PC hardware). As a result, although 20 percent of customer questions posed to a Bot may not be recognized or may be unanswerable, the response is immediate. For perhaps 80 percent of customers, an immediate response, canned or otherwise, is preferable to waiting on hold for 20 minutes to speak with a live representative.

The performance of a Bot can be improved by continually updating the responses and the possible questions that customers might pose to the Bot. Most of the commercial systems make this maintenance task tenable by saving queries that are not understood and presenting those to the maintenance staff in a format that makes updating the system straightforward. In addition, most Bots used in customer support pass the customer on to the queue of a customer service rep after two failed

IN THE REAL WORLD

Virtual Personalization

Lands' End's approach to personalization combines online three-dimensional rendering technology with a customer database to allow customers to create digital clones of themselves. Like virtual Barbie and Ken dolls, customers can try on the clothing from the online Lands' End catalog and visualize themselves wearing the products. The customer database, which is confidential, contains information such as hairstyle, skin tone, height, weight, inseam, and other personal physical characteristics used to construct the three-dimensional models.

attempts to handle the customer's question. In this way, customers are not left frustrated with their questions unanswered and with no human to turn to for help.

Virtual Customer Service Representatives

When it comes to a conversation, a face—and a facial expression—is worth a thousand words, in part because it adds a dimensionality. To this end, several companies, including Haptek and LifeF/X, offer three-dimensional animated "talking heads" that can be used as front ends to E-mail and CRM applications. When linked with one of the conversational Bots described earlier, and a text-to-speech (TTS) engine that converts text to spoken English, these virtual reps give the appearance of a real person who can discuss the customer's problem. That is, the Bot provides the "intelligence," the TTS engine provides the voice, and the virtual rep engine provides the three-dimensional character. Both the Haptek (www.Haptek.com) and LifeF/X (www.lifefx.com) sites offer free examples of these technologies.

KEY TERM

Text-to-speech (TTS) A technology based on the generation of spoken English (or other language), based on text input. The problem with most TTS systems or engines is that the sounds are somewhat mechanical and do not convey the subtle inflections of human speech, although today's computer voices are intelligible.

The realism of the virtual rep is enhanced by the three-dimensional appearance, the normal random blinking, roving eyes, and the lip-synched movements choreographed to the TTS output. The three-dimensional character can be a model or generated from a series of digital photos (front and side views) of someone in the company. The current limitation of this technology is that customers must have plug-ins or Web browser extensions loaded on their PCs in order to see the talking heads and hear the speech. Although the license arrangement with most plug-ins are such that developers pay fees and users have free use of the plug-ins, the plug-ins are typically several megabytes in size, making them too big to download through a slow dial-up connection.

In addition to use on the wired Web, companies are developing similar systems to enhance business through Wireless devices. For example, Eyematic Interfaces is working with Qualcomm, TRW, Omron, and other wireless companies to offer virtual rep technology over low-bandwidth cell phones. Instead of keying expressions to the text generated by a Bot, these systems use a camera to monitor facial expressions and instruct the virtual rep to replicate the expression on the customer's end. In this way, a realistic image of the customer support representative can be reproduced on the customer's low-bandwidth cell phone. That is, the system acts as a form of compression, allowing realistic video images to be used in communications, even though bandwidth limits don't allow actual video images. Unlike systems on the wired Web, these wireless applications are not yet commercially available; however, they clearly highlight the direction of the technology that will soon be available for eCRM.

Challenges

The Web brings many challenges as well as opportunities to the eCRM space. These challenges, listed in Figure 5-3, include those associated with CRM in general, as well as several Web-specific issues. For example, there is the usual challenge of identifying vendors and consultants, but the challenge is highlighted because of the lack of vendors with extensive backgrounds in eCRM. Most of the market leaders have only a few years of experience in the space. For example, Oracle, although firmly established in the database market and well known in the CRM space, is still evolving its eCRM offerings. In comparison, most CRM vendors have even less experience on the Web.

FIGURE 5-3	
Challenges	**Issues**
Bandwidth Limitations	Do customers have sufficient connectivity?
Business Analysis	Investment requirements vs. unknown return
Business Model	New models needed
Computer Penetration	Extent of the computer as a touch point
Customer Preferences	Will they use the PC?
Development	Internal or outsourced?
Employee Motivation	May resist automation
Evolving from CRM to eCRM	Cost, time, and vision
Evolving Standards	Web is volatile
Gamers	Customers may game the system
Hardware Requirements	New call center equipment needed
Identifying Vendors	Most vendors are new to the space
More Data	Larger databases, more data to deal with
New Integration Issues	How to integrate E-commerce data with other data?
Security and Privacy	The Web is less secure than other touch points
Training	Cost and scheduling

From the perspective of corporate culture, employee motivation and training are two major challenges to face before a company can successfully use eCRM. For one thing, employees may feel threatened by the prospect of losing their jobs to a new computer-based system. For less extensive systems that rely on customer reps for operation, there is the issue of training. Not only is the cost of training a factor, but if there is high rep turnover—as is normal in the industry—it may also be difficult to maintain a trained staff if new reps must be trained in basic computer operation before they can be productive.

From a business perspective, adding a Web touch point to a CRM initiative is fraught with challenges. There is the cost of additional computer hardware and software, including maintenance. In addition, this outlay may not result in a significant ROI, and lost opportunity costs may be substantial as well. After everything is in place, it may be that customers eschew the Web as a touch point and that the money could have gone farther by adding additional customer service reps, for example. Although the Web is a useful touch point, for some customers and for some products, the telephone or personal service may be more appropriate. While the Web seems like an obvious touch point for CRM related to computer products and technology in general, a customer who has problems with his or her new car is likely to prefer the telephone or personal contact. In other words, eCRM is more appropriate for products and services that are themselves connected to computers and the Web or that don't need a high degree of intimacy or assurance from the customer service representative. For example, it's hard enough to get a mechanic to promise to repair a car on a specified date in person, much less through an E-mail.

From a technical perspective, eCRM has the potential of creating more data than other touch points; however, the issue is how to handle vast amounts of data that can be automatically captured from the Web. Practical issues range from managing larger databases to the cost of archiving the data. There is also the issue of how to deal with data created by customers who intentionally game the system. For example, customers may complain about a product or service in order to obtain coupons, rebates, discounts on future purchases, or simply to enter a contest multiple times.

Future of CRM and eCRM

As the Web becomes less distinguishable from other touch points, eCRM will meld with CRM. The issue today is that the two are viewed as different methods by vendors competing for the eCRM space. These companies typically offer products for CRM based on traditional computer architectures that are in some degree of transition to Web-based systems. In the short term, as competition grows in the eCRM arena, and some products and services are disrupted because of acquisitions, mergers, and failures, there will be increased volatility, and potential for customer frustration. As customers and companies become more comfortable with the Web as a touch point, however, eCRM will cease to exist as a separate entity. Like the telephone or the fax, the Web will become just another CRM touch point.

Summary

The Web has several characteristics that make it ideally suited to CRM, from immediacy and flexibility to popularity and self-documentation. CRM over the Web is called eCRM. One of the issues with the Web relative to eCRM is that many customers have inflated expectations of what the touch point can deliver today; however, given the range of evolving technologies that can be applied to eCRM, from data warehousing to Bots and virtual customer representatives, these expectations may soon be met. Within a few years, the Web-specific components of CRM, like the telephone, will be considered a part of every CRM initiative. Chapter 6 explores how the Web and other technologies can be realistically evaluated for their use in CRM today.

The universe is full of magical things, patiently waiting for our wits to grow sharper.

Eden Philpotts

CHAPTER 6

Evaluating Solutions

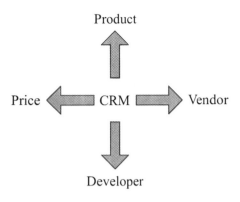

Product

Price ⟸ CRM ⟹ Vendor

Developer

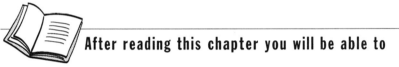

After reading this chapter you will be able to

- Evaluate the various software solutions to CRM
- Navigate successfully in a volatile, changing CRM industry
- Predict the trajectory of the major CRM software developers

A CEO who is challenged to implement or expand a CRM initiative has to come to grips with several issues. The first is how to evaluate software, developers, and vendors in a volatile market during a time of rapidly changing technology. Then there are the economics of the situation (explored in depth in Chapter 7), the culture of the corporation that will be affected by the CRM initiative, and the technology used in the implementation. Remember that CRM is a process that can use computer software and other technologies to increase the likelihood of success in keeping profitable customers and improve the overall bottom line. Thus it is more than a software program, call center, or sales and marketing tool.

Developer The creator of a software product (e.g., Microsoft and Oracle).

Vendor The seller of software products. Vendors are typically value-added resellers of products that may be bundled with other products and services, such as training. In some cases, the vendor and developer are one company.

In most cases, the technology is inextricably tied to one or two CRM software vendors who either developed it or introduced it to the CRM space; however, no two CRM software vendors or developers are identical, and the solutions they offer typically differ in significant ways. In addition, the differences may not be readily apparent. Differentiating among vendors and technology solutions is complicated because of the rapid pace of technologic evolution of CRM software, as discussed in Chapters 4 and 5. Even so, CEOs can apply metrics—perhaps more aptly described as heuristics or common-sense tips—to CRM solutions to better their odds of success. As illustrated at the beginning of this chapter, these metrics include the characteristics of the product, price, and the status of the vendor and developer.

As illustrated in the continuing story of the bike shop, a CEO has to be flexible and cautious in embracing any of the evolving CRM solutions. In particular, as the discussion following the story illustrates, the CEO should be aware of the tradeoffs associated with selecting one solution over another, as well as how to recover from the inevitable bumps along the road (including vendor failure) in any technology-related initiative.

🚲 Unexpected Challenges

Life is good for Hank. Profits are up at his bike shop, in part because of his recent CRM effort, which he ties directly to marketing and sales initiatives. The shop is buzzing along, especially since Debra installed several software packages that help Hank create brochures for sales and marketing campaigns, keep track of payroll expenses, and manage other business-related tasks. Because Debra chose software that was easy to learn and work with, Hank and his assistants are able to use the computer system and even create some of the Web site materials without her help.

Unfortunately, several of the ancillary software packages installed on Hank's computer system are out of date. Because the contact management software requires an older version of the operating system than do the updates for the other programs that Hank uses every day, Hank can't upgrade to the latest version of the operating system. The developer of the contact management software has promised an upgrade compatible with the latest operating system for more than six months now, but it hasn't materialized. As a result, Hank can't install or use the features of the latest operating system, and he can't install bug fixes and other improvements that would ostensibly increase his efficiency.

About a year after Debra first installed the contact manager software on Hank's computer, the company that developed the software is acquired by a competing company. Because the new company's plans for the contact manager software product aren't certain, Debra suggests that changing to a new contact management program that is compatible with the latest version of the operating system is probably the wisest choice. If he stays with the current software, Hank won't be able to upgrade his computer system to use the latest version of the Web browser and a variety of program updates that provide increased functionality that he really needs in his business.

Debra and Hank decide to proactively address the potential demise of their current contact management software by exporting the customer data to another, more stable product. Debra's challenge is to identify the product that most closely fulfills Hank's needs and that is most likely to survive the next five years—at the high end for the expected life of the software. As such, Debra uses a variety of metrics to evaluate products and vendors. She looks at the form and function of the software, the flexibility of the system and of the vendor, the market focus, the service contract, price, and references. She also looks at the data formats and compatibility standards, ability to import and export data from and to a variety of industry-standard database engines, and the industry standing of the developer.

After evaluating several product brochures and write-ups and talking to owners of other bike shops in other cities, Hank and Debra identify a software package that appears to suit their needs. In addition, the company that developed the contact management part of the package appears to have a solid foothold in the CRM space. Their marketing materials indicate that their CEO has a vision of the future that includes the Web, wireless, and other touch points that Hank may eventually want to exploit. Convinced it's the best move, Hank orders the contact management system. Because it's a shrink-wrapped product, the software arrives ready to install in less than a week.

Because there's no need to change over to the new system immediately, Debra introduces it slowly to Hank and his assistants over a month of weekly training sessions. Fortunately, the old and new systems are similar, and she doesn't have to go into the details of how to use the computer hardware. There are some differences in how the new operating system looks and responds, but the difference is a matter of degree, and easily learned. After Hank and his assistants have been trained on the new system, Debra switches everything over to the new contact management program and the other program updates. In all, it takes Hank's team about two months to feel comfortable with the new system. Although Hank would have preferred to not have invested in a company destined for failure, he accepts the investment in the initial CRM package as a learning process. In addition, Debra now feels better equipped to evaluate CRM software products and companies, and computer software companies in general, than she was before the incident.

Solution Selection

Fortunately for Hank, the cost of a new CRM software package was only a few hundred dollars, and training Hank and his assistants wasn't a lengthy, arduous process. For a company with dozens of customer support reps, a dozen or more salespeople, and several marketing specialists, however, upgrading or switching to a new CRM software package can involve significant corporate resources.

In many instances, the presence of a legacy system impedes the progress of installing a new system. Not only must the existing system be operated and maintained while the new system is being installed and configured, but switching over to the new system may also involve disrupting the entire call center for several days. Not only must those in the IS department deal with the issues of transferring data from the legacy system to the new system, but customer service reps must be trained on the new system as well. For larger call centers, simply scheduling training classes for customer service reps may be a significant challenge to overcome.

One approach to selecting a CRM product is to simply hire a consultant to analyze the needs of the company, pick a product and a vendor, and oversee the project implementation. The other approach is to use in-house resources. In either case, the corporate CIO should be intimately involved in the process. It also makes sense for the CEO to limit the company's exposure by taking part in the evaluation process. Clearly, the best approach to avoiding Hank's situation with a moribund developer is to carefully evaluate the CRM developer in the first place. Had Debra known about the volatility of the CRM field, she could have looked at the developer's market share, track record of the officers of the company, and the financial status of the company to assess the stability of the developer.

Just as Debra is new to the CRM field, so are many consultants, simply because it's a new and rapidly expanding space that attracts many consultants with expertise in other areas. This means the initial selection of a CRM solution should be based on careful consideration of as much information as is practical. In this regard, the CRM software should be evaluated in terms of both a software product and as a specific CRM solution. That is, there are desirable characteristics common to every software product, from adequate documentation and freedom from bugs to ease of use and support for peripherals, such as printers. CRM-specific attributes include the ability to support CRM processes, from tracking customer complaints to mining customer data for hidden relationships. Similarly, the developer and the vendor should be evaluated in terms of their likely business and product viability in the CRM space.

CRM Product Evaluation

Figure 6-1 lists some of the major criteria to consider in evaluating a CRM product in terms of a CRM solution. Obviously, the majority of work for this assessment will be the responsibility of either the CIO or an external consultant; however, the CEO needs to have an understanding of the concepts involved in CRM product evaluation regardless of who performs the actual evaluation. The evaluation of a product as a CRM solution focuses on product and price, as described in the following sections.

FIGURE 6-1

Product

Add-On Availability/Cost/Terms
Availability
Benefits
Compatibility with Existing System
Compatibility with Internal Processes
Compatibility with Other Systems
Documentation Quality and Availability
Features
Functionality
Growth Path
Installed User Base
Intended Application
Intended Audience
Interface Cost/Availability
Legacy Data Transfer Utilities
Localization Options
Missing Components
Performance
Performance/Response Time
Reliability
Specialized or Bundled
Telecom Compatibility
Training Availability/Cost
User's Group/Newsletter/Publications

Price

Cost of Upgrades
License Arrangements
Price/Volume Discounts

Product

The most critical component of the solution evaluation is to focus on the current availability of the advertised product, and not what's promised "any day now." It may be tempting to go with a major developer that promises to evolve its current offering into a product that will eventually provide a spectrum of impressive features and functions; however, there is a significant risk that the developer may never deliver on its promise or may introduce a product late—months or even years in the future. Because many companies announce a product before it's actually available for sale in order to claim market share, the CEO should determine if the expected delivery timeline is accurate.

One of the many advantages of considering an actual product is that it and the often overlooked peripheral service and products can be directly evaluated. For example, what is the quality and availability of user and administrator documentation? Are there versions geared toward various types of users (e.g., one for sales, one for marketing, and one for call center employees)? Is the documentation up to date, or does it lack information on the latest products?

Another advantage of evaluating a shipping product is that the size and nature of the installed user base can be evaluated. Is the size of the user base in line with the length of time the product has been shipping? A smaller than expected user base may suggest that either the company isn't very good at marketing or other companies have passed over the product for various reasons. Perhaps the product is excellent, but training availability is limited or the cost is prohibitive. Similarly, the developer and affiliated vendors may have failed to provide newsletters, start users' groups, or initiate other activities that can help new customers solve the inevitable problems that crop up during installation and use.

Evaluating the current product's functionality, features, and benefits from the perspective of a CRM solution should include comparing the company's needs with what the product offers. For example, is there a sales force automation component to the software, and does it provide the functionality needed by the sales department? If not, is there a proven, compatible product that can provide the missing functionality, and if so, at what cost? Is the product an add-on from the same company or is it from a third party? Is the add-on available now, and what's the status of the third party as a business?

Evaluating the list of features that a CRM product provides requires a knowledge of what's generally accepted as the norm for the type of product being evaluated. For example, the feature set for an enterprise-wide contact management system might include:

- Number of custom reports that can be generated
- Maximum number of users that can be supported by a networked system
- Flexibility of the database search engine
- Query power and ease of use
- Compatibility with add-ons from other developers
- Minimum hardware requirements
- Support for special hardware, such as auto-dialers
- Compatibility with various versions of the most popular operating systems

The intended audience and application for the product should match the requirements of the company's domain. Although a CRM product that is designed to be used in a medical setting may be able to be used in manufacturing, it may not be the best fit. It's usually better to find a product that has been developed to work effectively in the same area it was designed for because of small details that can make a system either useful or unusable. A medical enterprise, for example, may need a system that tracks customer (patient) insurance information and automatically forwards it to an affiliated pharmacist along with prescription orders. This type of functionality will not be included with a system designed to track the status of customer orders in a manufacturing facility.

In addition to selecting a product developed for the right domain, a product designed for the intended audience is important for internal buy-in. For example, if a CRM product is call center–centric and doesn't provide sales or marketing with the functionality they need, or requires them to change their current way of doing business, then those in sales and marketing may kill the initiative. Conversely, if the product is sales-centric, providing efficient and effective support for the sales process, then marketing and call center employees may reject the product. Most devastating, in terms of time, money, and wasted effort, is when the rejection of the system because it doesn't support existing processes becomes obvious only after the system is installed.

In addition to gaining departmental acceptance, the CRM product may have to be compatible with existing software and hardware systems. As such, compatibility with current telecom systems may be a deciding factor, especially if the budget won't handle new telecom hardware or software upgrades. Similarly, as in the story, the product should be compatible with the latest operating system offerings, regardless of the hardware platform.

Product performance, in terms of response time, and reliability in the intended application area are obvious requirements. Functionality, features, and price are irrelevant if salespeople or customer service reps have to wait on a slow system or one that is frequently down because of bugs or other problems. Similarly, if the system is intended to create happy, repeat customers, then a system that extends their wait time is not going to prove beneficial. The solution should improve throughput and decrease time wasted on tasks not directly related to customer support.

If the corporation is international and/or deals with customers who speak multiple languages. then localization options will be important. For example, even if customers are limited to the United States, many of them may prefer to speak Spanish. If the goal is to increase customer satisfaction among users who prefer alternatives to the English language, then provision for alternatives to English language E-mail, Web, and computer-generated speech marketing materials should be considered.

Working with existing systems and data may require interfaces to the system or utilities that can import the legacy data into the new system. If the legacy system is destined for decommissioning, then legacy data transfer utilities or export should be available. These utilities can be bundled with the product or they can be available as third-party add-ons.

Interface development is one of the most challenging, time-consuming, and expensive areas in computer system development, in or out of the CRM world. System-to-system interface development is a multibillion-dollar business worldwide, with most in-house information service departments spending at least one-quarter of their effort developing interfaces between new systems and between new and legacy computer systems. In most cases, interface development will be handled by a third party, even if only subcontracted out by the CRM product vendor.

Given the rapid rate of growth and evolution of the CRM space, the extensibility of a CRM product may be a critical factor. If no obvious growth path is available, then upgrading to a more capable system may require throwing out the existing one and going with a new product altogether, as Hank did in the story. If the company does offer a growth path, what are the costs and licensing terms? Similarly, what is the compatibility of this future product with currently installed systems or systems that may be under consideration? (i.e., if a suite of tools is being considered, each focused on a different area of CRM, what are the integration issues? Is there a track record for the combination under consideration?)

Finally, getting employees up to speed on a product requires training, either in-house or off-site, depending on the location and cost of training options. Similarly, the quality and nature of documentation can be critical. Online documentation is especially important for employees on the move, such as outside salespeople, who can't be expected to lug a thick user's manual around with them on business trips.

Price

Price is always an issue. The licensing terms have to be in line with the reality of the marketplace and what the company can afford. In general, products that follow the application service provider (ASP) model are less expensive in the short-term than are software products that have to be loaded and maintained locally. Most ASP vendors use a subscription model in which the software and all updates are available through a standard Web browser. Although there may be an initial customization cost, the initial outlay for an ASP-based approach is generally significantly less than the license for local installation. Another price issue is related to upgrades. Again, the ASP model normally includes upgrades, which typically occur in the background and may not even be noticeable to users.

When discussing licensing terms, aim to understand the total cost for the company. Does the price for a site license include an unlimited number of copies or is it limited to a fixed number of copies that can be used internally and off-site—for offsite sales, for example? Is the maintenance contract reasonable and affordable? Finally, the company should have an exit strategy—a predefined means of ending the relationship—

if it decides to divest itself of the CRM product and invest its money elsewhere. In this regard, licensing and contractual terms should allow the company freedom to continue with the relationship if it's in its best interest to do so.

Software Evaluation

In addition to the CRM-specific components of product evaluation, every software product can and should be evaluated on a set of application-independent criteria, including those listed in Figure 6-2.

FIGURE 6-2

Software Evaluation Criteria

Automatic Analysis of Unauthorized Use Attempts
Documented Nature of Failures
Ease of Use
Established Mechanism for Bug Reporting and Fixes
Export/Import to/from Popular Formats
Generous Warranty/Guarantee
Graphical User Interface
Nonproprietary Software Architecture
Number of Failures
Number of Successful Installations
Number of Successful Installations In Operation
Operating System Certification
Reasonable Maintenance Contract
Reasonable Update Frequency
Reasonable, Articulated Growth Path
Security Levels and Access
Standard Database Engine
Standard Distribution Media
Standard Hardware Requirements
Standard Network Compatibility
Standard Operating Environment
Standard Operating System Requirements
Standard Peripherals Supported
Time-Limited Passwords

The most important criterion is adherence to standards, which is reflected in operating system and hardware compatibility. Unfortunately, in the software world standards are seldom fixed for more than a few months before they are updated. As such, evaluating current standards and projecting how long they will survive is an art that involves futuristic predictions about how operating systems, hardware, and other software products will evolve to address current deficiencies and future challenges. A product that requires custom, nonstandard computer hardware and obsolete or proprietary networking software and hardware is a risk, regardless of the functionality it provides.

The importance of software standards extends from the distribution media, peripherals supported, and database engine to the software architecture and data formats. For example, if the software is distributed on a certain format of magnetic tape, it may be difficult for a small IS shop to install the upgrades without purchasing a particular tape drive. In this case, a CD-ROM would be a better distribution media.

Adhering to standards usually confers some degree of interoperability—an ability to run on different hardware and under different operating systems. For example, if the CRM product is based on a standard database engine, such as Oracle, Ingress, or Sybase, then readily available database tools can be used to move data into and out of the system. This interoperability is time-limited because data formats may evolve to noncompatible standards, even within the same product line.

In contrast, if a nonstandard, proprietary database engine and format are used as the basis for a CRM application, the data may be effectively trapped in the application unless there is some means of exporting data in standard formats. Many software developers decide too late to move over to established standards or err in picking a standard to follow. Unfortunately for developers and their customers, the consequences of this seemingly inconsequential error can be devastating. Redesigning a software system can be so resource intensive that the company may lose commercial viability.

When it comes to adherence to standards, it takes more than a salesperson's claim of compatibility. Such claims should be backed up by official certificates of compatibility with the manufacturer of the computer and network operating systems. For example, a software product that is certified as compatible with Microsoft NT—as signified by the Microsoft insignia on the product packaging—has to fulfill criteria established by Microsoft. Lack of official certification means that the developer either didn't take the time to submit the software for certification or the product failed the certification process.

Since the introduction of the Apple Macintosh and the Windows operating system, developers and vendors have claimed ease of use thanks to intuitive graphical user interfaces.; however, most CRM data are typically textual, and having a graphical user interface doesn't necessarily confer ease of use on a program. Make every effort to determine, from a user's perspective, the ease of use of a CRM program. This information can be garnered by interviewing actual users of the program or through unbiased reviews of the product in trade journals that compare and rank products in a specific category against objective criteria.

Related to ease of use are the training requirements. Determine how many hours of training are recommended before representatives in sales, marketing, and customer support can begin introducing database changes in the software effectively.

In assessing a developer and its products, determine the number of successful installations and how many of these successful installations are in operation. The CRM field is infamous for having large, "successful" installations that are for the most part ignored by employees. In other words, many companies are sitting on "successful" CRM installations that aren't in operation. For customers who have failed, determine the nature of their failure. Was it because of defects in the software or because it was the wrong product for the task at hand? Are there any similarities in the failed sites that suggest the product may fail in the planned installation as well?

What is the nature of the maintenance contract? Is it based on a fixed percentage of the initial contract value (typically 30 percent) or is it billed on a per-minute basis? What is the update frequency? Although software warranties are characteristically one-sided, with the developer offering to replace defective tapes, CD-ROMs, or other media, is there something in the warranty worth considering, such as free support for the first quarter of operation?

A reasonable, articulated growth path differentiates software designed for short-term gains and uncertain futures from CRM solutions that can grow with the needs and vision of the company. For example, if a networked contact management system that is sold for small workgroups of up to 20 reps can be upgraded to an enterprise-grade system that supports up to 200 reps, a growth path is available to customers as well. Developers with products that can grow with the needs of the company are a much safer bet in the long term.

Finally, understand the provisions for security. Time-limited passwords that require representatives to change their passwords every three or four months are a plus. Similarly, software that supports multiple levels of security and access is mandatory in large installations where individual representatives can easily hide their identity.

Developer Evaluation

The purchase of a software license from a developer marks the beginning of a partnership. From the CEO's perspective, the major question is whether the partnership has the potential to be a lasting one or is destined to be a short-term affair with an exchange of money for product and a short business horizon.

Whereas software product evaluation may necessarily fall under the purview of the CIO, developer evaluation clearly falls on the shoulders of the CEO. Developer evaluation entails looking at the developer from a strictly business perspective. The developer simply happens to be making software instead of some widget. From this perspective, the goal of developer evaluation is to determine the viability of the developer, using some of the criteria listed in Figure 6-3.

FIGURE 6-3

Developer Evaluation Criteria

Bank References	Market Share
CEO/CFO Qualifications	Number of Clients
Company Profile	References
Consultant Impressions	Software Escrow Availability
Focus	Viability
History	Vision for Future Products
Independent Product Reviews	Write-ups

Just as in any other mission-critical business arrangement, choose a CRM developer carefully, starting with the qualifications of upper-level management. Relevant questions to ask are: What is the CEO's track record? Does the CEO of the company in question have experience in the CRM space? What about in the domain that the product will be used in? How long has the CEO and other upper-level management been in place? If a consultant is involved with the evaluation, what is his or her subjective impression of the company overall and of the management team in particular? A consultant who has worked with upper level-management in the CRM field may be able to easily rate the relative worth of a particular team.

Developers with CEOs and management teams that fall in the "quick turnaround" category represent more of a risk than those who specialize in long-term growth. Turnaround CEOs typically spend one or two years getting a company back on its feet in preparation for a corporate acquisition. Although the result may be optimum for stockholders, an acquisition often means that the future of the CRM product is uncertain and depends on the vision of the acquiring company. On one hand, an acquisition may result in a much stronger product, bolstered by the finances and marketing muscle of a much larger investor. On the other hand, the acquisition may be by a competitor who wants to extract some key technologies or intellectual property rights from the company or simply keep the competition off the market, but has no need to maintain the CRM products. Perhaps the best known example of this sort of maneuvering in the business world is VisiCalc.

Even though VisiCalc was the first commercially available spreadsheet on the microcomputer, Lotus was able to move its 1-2-3 product from number two to number one in the spreadsheet market by acquiring VisiCalc and simply removing it from the market. As a result, the CRM software won't be updated to follow advances in operating systems, and third-party developers may abandon the product in favor of developing utilities and add-ons for CRM systems from other companies.

In addition to quality and focus of upper-level management, the other major indicator of developer viability is the company's financial health. In this determination, bank references that show capital on hand, outstanding loans, and other economic indicators should be reviewed. If the company is public, then this information is readily available. If the company is privately held, then the information should be available with the appropriate nondisclosure agreements in place. Developers that don't want to comply with disclosure requests shouldn't be considered.

Is the developer's company economically viable? The developer's market share of the CRM pie is a good indicator of future viability. Determine if the developer's market share is increasing, decreasing, or stable. If market share is rapidly increasing, can the company reasonably be expected to service existing accounts while in an expansion mode? If it's decreasing, is there an external reason, such as a downturn in the economy or the emergence of a new competitor? Or is the reason internal, such as misdirection by upper-level management? How many clients does the developer have, and how many of these are long-term? In a related issue, how much of the developer's revenues are the result of business from its top two or three clients? If the top one or two companies account for more than half of the developer's revenues, then the developer is potentially unstable, especially if the top investors are likely to be volatile (e.g., they're dotCom companies).

A developer's focus and heritage can provide insight into its most probable future directions. A huge company with a variety of products that includes one or more CRM solutions among other offerings may suggest stability, but the variety of products to maintain and update may siphon resources from the CRM products. The heritage of the company, whether from the database, sales force automation (SFA), or enterprise resource planning (ERP) arenas, gives a good indication of where the company is headed and where its strengths and weaknesses may lie.

For example, a database company that is entering the CRM space probably has a broader understanding of the infrastructure and interconnectivity issues related to the long-term viability of any CRM initiative than does a company with an SFA heritage. In contrast, a company with

KEY TERM

Enterprise resource planning (ERP) The category of software designed to improve the internal processes of a company.

a successful background in SFA probably has a good understanding of the importance of involving end-users in application design; the interdependencies of sales, marketing, and call center staff; and of the CRM space in general. If the developer has an SFA pedigree, however, it may not be the best company to support a call center–centric operation because of a lack of experience with call centers. Companies entering the CRM space from the ERP world, in which internal business processes are examined to pinpoint and correct deficiencies, are likely to have a good knowledge of infrastructure and end-user requirements.

If the developer has been around for more than a few months, a significant installed user base, positive references, and a company-sponsored user's group, newsletter, or other publications all contribute to the status of a CRM developer; however, someone has to be the early adopter of a new technology. If the developer is new to CRM and therefore potentially unstable, then the developer must be willing to establish a software escrow account. As described earlier, a software escrow account allows companies that partner with the developer to access the CRM product source code if the developer fails in the marketplace.

Third-party write-ups should be examined as well. Are the independent product reviews and trade magazine write-ups consistently positive? If not, are the factors considered negative significant to the company's relationship? Finally, determine whether the developer's vision of the future of CRM is compatible with the goals of the partnering company. A company that envisions itself moving rapidly into the wireless Web space shouldn't partner with a developer that sees itself as a PC-based application for the foreseeable future.

Vendor Evaluation

The vendor—the actual seller of a CRM product—represents the local personality of the developer. As such, the evaluation of the vendor is

TIPS & TECHNIQUES

CRM Vendor References

Selecting a CRM vendor is a lot like getting married—or at least moving in together. It's strategically imperative to learn as much as possible about the vendor before money changes hands. In this regard, the direct experience of previous clients can be invaluable, even if the list of references is provided by the CRM vendor. Key questions to ask companies provided as references by the CRM vendor include:

- What's the company's experience with CRM vendors on specific issues? Avoid generalities and ask specific, quantifiable questions, such as the average phone call response time and the number of problems that came up during installation and the time to resolve each problem.

- Is this the company's first CRM initiative? In general, customers who have been burned once by a CRM vendor provide better information than those who have tried once and succeeded.

- How long ago was the relationship with the current CRM vendor started? Many facets of support and the overall relationship become evident only after the initial honeymoon period is over.

- What were the problem areas? Note that there are always problem areas, and for a company to state otherwise is a giveaway that the reference shouldn't be trusted.

- Is the company being compensated in any way for a positive reference? For example, does the company own stock in the CRM vendor or do they share a common funding source?

- Would the company use the same CRM vendor in the future?

- Does the company know of situations in which the CRM vendor failed?

- What was the company's second vendor of choice? Why? Check out this vendor as well.

TIPS & TECHNIQUES CONTINUED

Obviously, CRM vendors offer references that are mostly positive; however, selecting a CRM vendor, like picking the right spouse or roommate, is a personal matter. Issues that may not be important to one company may be paramount to another. For example, a company given as a reference may give high marks on technical support, only because its internal IS staff was able to solve most of the inevitable problems without calling for help. For a company without an extensive, well-trained IS group, however, vendor technical support will have much more significance in the buy decision.

closely linked to that of the developer, especially when the vendor and developer share product, vision, and sometimes even people. Figure 6-4 lists the major criteria to consider in evaluating a CRM product vendor. Although the vendor and developer can be the same entity, most developers concentrate on developing product and establish relationships with vendors who can focus on sales and marketing.

Because the vendor or value-added reseller (VAR) is really the only point of contact that a company has to the developer, the qualitative components of the relationship should be heavily weighted. For example, what is the style of the vendor, and is it compatible with the corporate culture? That is, is the extent of the vendor's involvement a series of PowerPoint presentations or is the vendor willing and able to help with internal sales and marketing of their product? Will they commit to being intimately involved with the kickoff of the CRM product, or will they be off selling to another company once a deal is made?

On a more quantitative note, how long has the vendor been in the CRM business, how many local clients does it have; and what are their experiences? Vendor qualifications should be verified by contacting the

---

FIGURE 6-4

Vendor Evaluation Criteria

Customization Policy	Relationship Builders
Developer-Certified	Reputation
Help with Internal Marketing	Style Compatibility
Involved in Kickoff	Support Options
Location	Time in Business
Number of Clients	Training Options

---

developer. Foremost in this determination is verifying that the vendor is certified as an official representative of the CRM product by the developer. Official vendor status is a prerequisite to receiving proper service, training, and warranty support. Another quantitative measure is the number of clients served by the vendor. Are there several in the area or is the contract under consideration the vendor's first? If it's the first, then there is the risk of not having support in the area when the company initiating a CRM effort needs it.

A related issue is the vendor's location. Having the vendor nearby is critical, especially during the startup and kickoff phases of a CRM initiative. How far do support personnel live from the vendor, and how often are the support and training personnel in the area? Assuming that the vendor's staff is local is a common mistake today. Many "virtual" companies outsource staff or allow them to commute to the main office only when necessary. If the support and training staff live in another state, response time in the event of emergencies will likely be compromised.

When it comes to responsiveness and support, what are the options? (i.e., what is the vendor's own CRM like?) Does the vendor provide walk-in, phone, E-mail, and telephone support, or simply E-mail? For an on-site visit, what is the guaranteed response time? Does the vendor offer off-site support via remote dial-in modem? Does support include on-site or off-site training? The correct answer to each of these ques-

Results May Vary

Most CRM initiatives take a year or more before any real change can be expected in the company's bottom line; however, there are exceptions. Hard Rock Cafe International invested in a CRM solution with the hopes of increasing the frequency of visits of regular patrons in its 104 restaurants. The Orlando-based company uses a CRM package to generate a list of E-mails to encourage customers to visit the restaurant and the corporate Web site, which offers souvenirs. Hard Rock Cafe was able to recoup most of its CRM investment in less than a year.

tions depends on the needs of the company and its budget for CRM. For example, a two-hour response time may be acceptable for a low-volume call center, but unacceptable for a high-volume center that caters to the needs of exemplary customers.

In evaluating a vendor, consider if the local vendor represents one solution or a variety of CRM products. The advantage of a vendor that represents only one CRM developer is that the staff is likely to have an in-depth understanding of the product, but the vendor's staff may also try to fit the product into all problems. In contrast, a vendor that represents CRM products from a variety of competing or complementary developers may have staff with less knowledge about any given product but may be able to recommend the best CRM solution from a wide range of available options.

Major Players

CRM is one of the most rapidly growing areas in the computer field. The explosive growth in demand for workable CRM solutions is creating a vacuum that is pulling in companies that traditionally specialize in databases, SFA, and ERP companies. For example, SalesLogic and Remedy/Applix come from the SFA space, and SAP, Oracle, Baan, and PeopleSoft have ERP pedigrees. Some of the companies listed in Figure 6-5 are developing CRM solutions *de novo,* whereas others are shortening time to market through strategic acquisitions. In the latter case, companies are leveraging their existing customer contacts in entering the CRM space. For example, the telecommunications hardware company Alcatel entered the CRM fray by acquiring CRM software developer Genesys.

FIGURE 6-5

Major CRM Companies

Alcatel/Genesys	Mustang
Analysis	Nextel
Andersen Consulting	Nortel/Clarify
AT&T	Octane
Brightware	Onyx Software
Cambridge Technology Partners	Oracle
Cap General	Panasonic
Chrondiant Software	Pegasystems
Customer Analytics	Pivotal Software
Deloitte Consulting	PeopleSoft
EPhiphony	Polycom
Edify	PricewaterhouseCoopers
EGain	Prime Response
Epiphany	Quintus
GN Netcom	Remedy/Applix
Graham Technologies	SalesLogic
Hyperion Solutions	SAP
IBM Global Services	Saratoga Systems
ICL	SAS Institute
Kana Communications	Services
Lucent	Siebel Systems
Melita	Sony
Mosaix	Symantec

The major players in the CRM space are in flux, changing positions in the market with each new merger, acquisition, and major contracts; however, at the end of 2001, the top-tier companies, in terms of market share and growth, included Siebel Systems, Oracle, PeopleSoft, Onyx Software, and Clarify. Of these top players, Siebel Systems is clearly the front runner, with nearly 20 percent of the CRM market. Oracle, the database giant, is extending its expertise and contacts in the ERP field to CRM and has the advantage of easy integration with existing systems, given that those tools have been developed for Oracle's database product. PeopleSoft leveraged its position as a CRM specialist by acquiring Vantive, a major player in the declining ERP market. Clarify's position was bolstered when it was acquired by the networking giant Nortel Networks. Onyx Software strengthened its position in the eCRM space by acquiring Versametrix, a developer of Internet-based CRM solutions, and Market Solutions, a market automation provider.

In reviewing the list of companies in Figure 6-5, remember that sheer size and market share don't necessarily transfer to applicability for a particular company or area. For example, no developer has succeeded in providing a seamless enterprisewide solution to CRM. Most companies are working in niche areas, hoping to be a component of a total CRM solution. For example, Brightware, eGain, Mustang, Octane, and Pegasystems specialize in eCRM solutions. Symantec is focused on contact management software solutions to CRM.

As the companies listed in Figure 6-5 jostle for position and redefine the CRM space through their offerings, the CEO should keep an eye on the bottom line and critically evaluate the probable ROI. To this end, Chapter 7, "Economics of CRM," continues the discussion of solution selection from the perspective of the investment required for a CRM initiative and the probable return.

Summary

Customer relationship management software solutions should be evaluated in four ways:

1. As a CRM solution

2. As a software product

3. By developer status

4. By vendor status

A particular product should be evaluated in terms of how closely it fulfills your company's needs; however, the long-term viability of the developer and the likelihood that the local vendor will be available for support are at least as important in defining a solution. Selecting a CRM solution is complicated because the major players in the CRM field are jostling for position in the volatile, rapidly evolving space. To date, no vendor is capable of providing a seamless customer-to-company CRM solution that automates every internal and external process involved in sales, marketing, and call center operation. Regardless of whether the CEO will be intimately involved in the evaluation process, he or she should understand the criteria used by the company's CIO or external consultancy in determining which software solutions best fit the company's needs.

To select well among old things is almost equal to inventing new ones.

Nicolas Charles Trublet

155

CHAPTER 7

Economics of CRM

After reading this chapter you will be able to

- Understand the economics of the CRM market

- Identify the stakeholders in the CRM space

- Appreciate the investments associated with a typical CRM initiative

- Identify the major risks associated with implementing a CRM initiative

- Understand how timing entry or expansion into the CRM space can be critical for enhancing customer loyalty

This chapter is really about self-defense—ways of doing business during a time of huge change in technology, of mergers, acquisitions, globalization, when technology is giving us a vision of better tools to meet the needs of a changing business practice. New groupware, for example, that promises to provide hitherto unprecedented communication among geographically dispersed parts of a conglomerate has to be researched to see how the promised benefits fit a company's business needs, and whether new products made by new companies using new technology will prove viable for the next five years. This chapter explores areas you will need to consider before instituting a CRM initiative or change.

Since the boom and bust of the dotCom economy, developers, vendors, and venture capitalists in the high-tech sector have been searching for the next "new thing." High-bandwidth Internet connectivity appeared to be the next new thing, but lack of standards and excess capacity put many of these companies in the red, including Corning and Lucent. Another promising area is wireless Web connectivity, which is off to a steady start, especially in Asia; however, the fastest growing market appears to be in customer relationship management, especially on the Internet and the Web.

One purpose of this chapter is to highlight some of the more significant economic aspects of the CRM space, including a look at the stakeholders, investment requirements, and some of the risks associated with implementing a CRM initiative. In the stakeholder analysis, the primary stakeholders, hardware vendors, software vendors, and outside services, which are depicted as white ovals in the figure at the beginning of this chapter, stand to benefit from a CRM initiative. In contrast, the company's customer service reps, representatives in sales and marketing, customers, and the competition, depicted in gray, may benefit or suffer from an initiative, depending on how the implementation is accomplished and whether it will ultimately be successful. To illustrate, consider the stakeholders involved in the continuation of Hank's experience with the world of CRM.

Commencement

Debra is in her last semester at the university, and it's time for her to start interviewing for a job after graduation. She asks Hank for a recommendation, which he gladly agrees to write for her.

Based on her Web searches, conversations with her computer science professors at the university, and advertisements for positions in computer trade journals, she identifies four areas that seem poised for growth:

1. Customer relationship management

2. Computer games

3. Wireless Web

4. Genomics

Given her experience with Hank's bike shop and her education, she investigates the jobs in the CRM field. Debra discovers that there is high demand for three kinds of programmers:

1. Back-end integrators, who would write code that connects the data stored in existing or legacy systems with new CRM programs, so that a CRM program can import data on a different system to use it as if it were part of its own system

2. Front-end developers and interface designers, who would create the screens that customers interact with in order to get data into and out of databases

3. ASP developers who can work with the Web, databases, and networks to create eCRM applications that are rented or leased to their customers

In her preliminary investigations, Debra finds that the ASP developers offer the highest pay, probably because of the demand for eCRM solutions. She also discovers, in talking with alumni who graduated last year, that going with an ASP-based eCRM company is risky, given the high number of acquisitions, mergers, and outright failures of companies in the space. Even so, Debra decides to take her chances and signs on with an ASP developer on the West coast.

When Debra breaks the news to Hank that she'll be leaving the area, he's happy for her, but he's also concerned about his CRM system and Web site. Debra promises to find a student at the university who can keep up the Web site, preferably using the barter system Hank established with Debra. The local CRM software vendor will certainly be able to keep Hank informed on the latest releases of the CRM software, help him install the software updates, and train his assistants. Hank would prefer to find someone who he could consult for general advice on his system—someone not wedded to a particular product—but he can't afford a professional consultant. Debra is confident that she can probably find someone at the university who can maintain the Web site and keep an eye on developments in the CRM industry as well—and promises to keep in touch.

CRM Economy

While the enterprise relationship planning (ERP) sector and the growth of dotComs have slowed, the CRM space has experienced growth rates comparable to that of the wired Web of the late 1990s. Although there are none of the outrageous valuations associated with the dotCom boom, from 1998 to 2001, the CRM market has grown from about $2 billion to nearly $8 billion, with about half of that a result of spending on eCRM. Companies like Siebel Systems, PeopleSoft, and Oracle have experienced annual growth rates for their CRM products in the 50 to 100 percent range. Even many of the smaller vendors and developers are also experiencing double-digit growth at a time when dotComs are laying off employees. The projections of most of the companies in the CRM field suggest an increasing rate of growth, especially in eCRM, through 2003 (see Figure 7-1).

Although this rapid influx of companies from other specialties and consultants with little or no experience in the CRM space is resulting in confusion and a relatively high incidence of failed CRM projects, the competition is responsible for acceleration in innovation as well. Just as

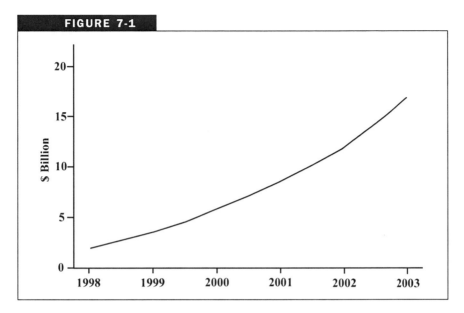

FIGURE 7-1

the influx of technical specialists and artists created a rich Web environment, a similar influx of skilled programmers and Web developers into
the space is resulting in a wealth of eCRM innovations. In the near term,
it isn't innovation, but rather the interoperability among the different
vendors that matters, at least until complete and affordable end-to-end
CRM solutions become available.

Stakeholders

The stakeholders in the CRM economy, illustrated in the stakeholder
analysis in the beginning of this chapter and listed in Figure 7-2, under-
line the link between CRM and the corporate employees, including
those in sales and marketing. Most of the failures in the CRM systems
that do make it past the numerous implementation hurdles are caused
by rejection of the systems by sales and marketing staff. For example, a
CRM system may work to specifications and even provide the call center with a more effective and more efficient means of collecting customer
data; however, if the sales force—often the major source of revenue for

the company —finds that the CRM system interferes with sales for any reason, it may kill the CRM initiative.

FIGURE 7-2

CRM Stakeholders

Advertising Agencies	CRM Vendors
Call Center	Legal Counsel
Company Employees	Marketing
Computer Hardware Vendors	Sales
Consultants	Telecom Hardware Vendors
Consulting Firms	Training Companies
CRM Developers	

Now, consider the customer as a stakeholder. The relevance of whether customers buy in to a new CRM system depends on the purpose of the system. If the goal is simply to fulfill state or federal legal requirements for providing support or even to discourage unprofitable customers from doing business with the company, then an inefficient system may be perfect for the company. Certainly, customers who have to wait on hold for a half hour in order to speak to a customer service rep aren't likely to do business with the company again in the near future.

Other important stakeholders in the CRM space come from those companies involved in supplying outside services. Consultants of all kinds are extremely influential in the economic success of CRM initiatives. As noted in Chapter 6, most CRM consultants learn on the job, given that demand for advice far exceeds the number of consultants with hands-on expertise in implementing successful CRM projects. As illustrated in the story, given the complex CRM space and the often bewildering array of choices available, seasoned and trusted advice can be invaluable. Similarly, most CEOs look to those with technical expertise in CRM to help make strategic decisions regarding CRM products and services.

Legal counsel also provides outside services. Given the volatility of the CRM space, it's imperative to secure product and service contracts that protect the company in the event that a CRM vendor, consultancy, or hardware company is acquired or otherwise unable to deliver on its promises. As noted in Chapter 6, a commonly used technique to ensure against being left stranded in the event of developer failure is to establish a software escrow account that includes source code, documentation, details of the development environment, and compiler instructions. In establishing a software escrow account, legal counsel can be key to stipulating requirements of the developer that guarantee that the source code is actually usable. For example, if the source code isn't updated immediately with each new software release, if there is no documentation on the code and how it is to be compiled, or if the programming environment isn't specified or provided, then the escrow account may be worthless. Similarly, without a detailed description of the development operating environment, including the version of the operating system, hardware requirements, the brands and configurations of the compilers and utilities required to convert the code into a usable application, the source code is practically useless.

There are simply too few people like Debra to go around, especially when it comes to training; however, the high-tech training industry has been quick to respond to the growing importance of CRM in the computer industry. Several of the larger training firms, such as the META Group and DGI, Inc., offer CRM training for executives and technology workers who need to come up to speed in the CRM field.

The various telecom and computer hardware manufacturers and their vendors obviously have a lot at stake in the success of CRM. Desktop PC sales in the United States are down, and margins are lower. Dell, IBM, and the other major computer hardware manufacturers are increasingly focusing on offshore sales, which are increasing. In the

United States, there simply isn't a compelling reason for most individuals or business owners to upgrade their PCs. Very few business applications demand processor speeds above 1 GHz or 500 MB of RAM. With no compelling reason for personal or business users to upgrade their arsenal of PCs, sales of desktop hardware are flattening; however, CRM initiatives are increasing the interest in new hardware, especially servers configured for ASP applications. Whether this increased interest in CRM will translate into demand for computer and telecommunications hardware and software remains to be seen.

Linked to the health of the major CRM-related computer hardware manufacturers and software developers is the fate of many advertising agencies and advertising services. Without significant activity in the CRM space, publishers won't be able to replace the flood of capital associated with the dotCom advertising blitz, and many magazines and trade journals will go from downsizing to demise. Fortunately for those in the advertising world, many of the major computer technology and business magazines regularly run features on CRM, and there is at least one regular magazine (*CRM,* published by Freedom Technology Media Group) dedicated to CRM. Several book publishers also have a stake in the CRM field, including those listed in the Further Reading section of this book, and the publisher of this book.

Investments

In order for each of the stakeholders to realize gains in the CRM space, each has to invest resources in kind. From the corporation's perspective, its employees in customer service, sales, marketing, and in other parts of the company have to make some or all of the investments listed in Figure 7-3 to benefit from a CRM initiative.

The return on investing in a CRM initiative is a customer-company relationship in which, as stated in Chapter 1, "customers elect to continue

FIGURE 7-3

Potential Corporate CRM Investments

Analysis	Hosting
Consultancy	Training
Computer Hardware	Programming
Telecommunications Hardware	License Fees
Software	Maintenance
Professional Services	Legal Counsel
Process	Lost Opportunity Costs
Marketing	Vendor Selection Process

mutually beneficial commercial exchanges and are dissuaded from participating in exchanges that are unprofitable to the company." With this goal in mind, some of the possible investments listed in Figure 7-3 are more significant than others.

Consider the research that goes into a typical CRM effort. It includes analysis of the corporate needs, vendor assessment and selection, and use of outside consultants if the estimate of lost opportunity costs shows such expenditure is warranted. The analysis of what the company needs is usually an iterative one in which the findings heavily influence what is considered necessary. In other words, analysis is interactive and iterative because, in performing the research, the research committee or consultant will probably discover a capability not considered possible or important before the research was begun. For example, marketing may not realize that a CRM program can provide data on how different age groups respond to particular marketing campaigns.

The initial interest in CRM may come about as a move to improve internal processes in general or as part of an ERP initiative. A CRM project may result from an analysis of how customers interact with the company or data from interviews with customer service, sales, or marketing staff. It may result from a cost analysis of handling customer complaints, the volume of complaints, and the nature of each complaint.

As noted in Chapter 6, selecting or at least qualifying a CRM vendor involves researching the background of the vendor, the developers they represent, and the various CRM products the vendor sells and supports. Directing corporate resources to research and implement a CRM initiative represents a cost in time, energy, and personnel. It also means that the resources are not available to apply to other challenges facing the company, so there is a lost opportunity cost as well.

Another area that demands investment is infrastructure. The CRM software is only one component of a new CRM solution, as defined in Chapter 5. In addition to creating a hardware and software infrastructure—the servers, cables, network operating system—there is the need to invest in the human infrastructure. For example, the sales force, marketing group, and customer service reps many have to be trained on how to use the CRM system most effectively.

Investing in external services is inevitable. Even the largest companies can't implement a comprehensive CRM solution in a timely manner on their own. For example, legal counsel is often critical in negotiating contractual agreements with CRM software vendors and developers. The need for legal support depends on the complexity of the CRM initiative, whether the task is to expand an existing CRM project or start a new one.

It may also be necessary to employ external marketing and process improvements consultants. Consider that if the CEO of a bank chain decides to implement an online banking system, the project may demand that the in-house marketing group mount an advertising campaign to convince customers of the benefit of using online banking, even though the initiative is intended to save on paper costs by eliminating the handling of checks, reducing the number of tellers, and offloading as much of the data entry task to customers.

Customers may be enticed to pay for the service in the name of saving time, even though online banking typically requires more of the customer's time than passing by an ATM on the way to work. In this regard, online banking also offloads the hardware investment from the bank to the customer. Instead of investing in an ATM for noncash transactions, such as account inquiries and transfers and paying bills, the customer pays for the hardware—the PC—and the Internet service provider (ISP) connect charges. With the proper marketing, customers can even be enticed to pay for the privilege of using online banking, one of the most active areas in E-commerce.

In addition to indirect costs for a CRM initiative, such as payroll expenses to pay for research, there are direct investments, such as software license fees, maintenance contracts, and per-minute or per-problem support fees. These costs vary considerably, depending on the nature of the software product and the number of users. Stand-alone, integrated contact management programs suitable for a small business like Hank's bike shop are available from about $200. The developer often provides free maintenance for the first 60 to 90 days and charges for support thereafter. Multiuser, enterprisewide versions of contact management software packages start off at about the same price per user, but are normally bundled in packs for five or six users. For more comprehensive CRM packages from one of the top vendors, the typical price per user is approximately $10,000.

To add to the investment in software is the cost of the server, networking hardware, and network operating system. Add to that the cost of a laptop for a mobile sales force, perhaps a wireless modem, and the monthly connection charges, and the initial per-user cost of an enterprisewide CRM system rises to the $12,000 to $15,000 range, not counting the annual maintenance fee (normally 30 percent of the software cost).

Adding to an existing CRM system can be less expensive than installing new PCs, servers, printers, and other hardware; however, even though starting from scratch can have a lower upfront cost, interfacing a new CRM software package to existing telecom hardware can be expensive and may take months to implement. Simply placing computers on the desks of customer service representatives can be expensive. Consider that the industrywide estimate for the annual cost of owning a PC in an office setting is about $5,000, which includes the initial cost of the hardware and the time lost getting everything up and running. There is also the ongoing cost of keeping the system running, including training new employees.

Risks

Despite the hype of CRM vendors, even the flawless execution of a CRM initiative may result in partial or total failure. That is, even if the typical hurdles associated with computerizing the processes of an organization can be avoided or overcome, internal and external factors can come into play; however, knowing what these hurdles are—as listed in Figure 7-4—can help the CEO recognize problems while they're insignificant or address likely issues before they arise.

FIGURE 7-4

Risks of CRM Implementation Failure

Vendor Failure	Internal Rejection
Customer Rejection	Evolving Standards
Cost Overruns	Shifting Customer Expectations
Time Overruns	General Economic Slowdown
Disruption of Service	New Technology

Most of the risks associated with implementing and realizing the potential benefits of a major CRM initiative can be categorized as either internal or external to the organization—and within or out of the CEO's direct control. For example, vendor failures, quickly evolving

---

KEY TERM

Disruptive technology A technology that empowers a different group of users and gets better over time. The PC is a disruptive technology, in that it empowered individuals to perform tasks once relegated to large data centers.

---

standards in the CRM marketplace, shifting customer expectations, the introduction of new, disruptive technologies that make the current implementation out of date before it's fully installed, and general economic slowdowns are largely uncontrollable.

Even so, due diligence in selecting a vendor, paying attention to the technological trajectory of the products offered by the top CRM developers and vendors, maintaining contact with customers and their wants and needs, and instructing the company's CIO or a consultant to stay abreast of potentially disruptive technologies can go a long way toward identifying external problems before they significantly impact the CEO's company. In addition, knowing the likely failure points can help avert disaster later. For example, given the volatility of CRM vendors, a second, backup vendor should be identified when the primary vendor is selected. The second vendor should be equipped to utilize a software escrow or to at least make use of the infrastructure so that the CRM project can continue with minimum disruption, should the first vendor fail.

Similarly, the negative effects of potentially disruptive technologies, such as the wireless Web, can be at least partially mitigated by selecting a CRM software developer with a forward vision and an R&D budget that includes experimenting with new technologies before they become mainstream. This developer should also have the means of bringing the technology to market. In other words, all else being equal, the CEO should make an effort to select the CRM software developer most likely to make the products from other CRM developers obsolete.

Related to software developer and vendor selection, as well as internal planning, whether with a consultancy or the internal IS department staff, are time and cost overruns, as well as the costs associated with disruption of service. Time and cost overruns, akin to those associated with virtually every government-funded construction project, such as Boston's Big Dig, can be minimized (or even avoided) by proper planning or by hiring a consultant who has actually implemented a CRM system and can therefore make realistic estimates. Industrywide, the cost of customization and integration of CRM software with other systems is the most expensive aspect of installation. Even small errors of omission or commission in the requirements and functional specifications that must be corrected later can significantly increase development expense and time requirements. Because most cost and time overruns are caused by the goal becoming a moving target (i.e., changes in the

---

KEY TERMS

Functional specifications The technical document that specifies exactly what a software and/or hardware system will deliver, in terms of response time, bandwidth, what data elements will be stored, exactly what each report contains, and other quantitative measures. A typical statement in a functional specification document would read "customer service representatives will be presented with the customer's prior purchases within 3 seconds of depressing the <F3> key."

Requirements specifications The qualitative document that specifies the needs that must be addressed by a particular technology. The requirements specification is written in language such as "the CRM system will allow marketing to sort customers by age."

TIPS & TECHNIQUES

Avoiding Disruption of Service

Disruption of service is one of the most costly risks associated with a CRM implementation. Leaving the legacy system in place and operational, dismantling it only after the new CRM system has been up and running satisfactorily for several months, can minimize the risk of disruption of service. The added cost of maintaining a dual system is inexpensive insurance.

specifications of the deliverable after the project has started), many of these overruns can be avoided by investing more resources into the planning stage of the project and not jumping into the implementation phase prematurely.

Perhaps the risk with the greatest potential for harm is unplanned disruption of service. Time overruns or unforeseen problems with implementation can result in costly disruptions in service that may, for example, leave the sales force without their normal connectivity to the main office. If a legacy system is removed so that a new CRM system can be put in place, the customer service reps, representatives in sales and marketing, and the customers are at the mercy of the CRM implementation team. Unfortunately, problems that should take a few days to fix often take months, leaving employees and customers without support. Disruption of service is most detrimental when the income-producing sales force is compromised because of a lack of connectivity to information they need to support the sales process.

These potential sources of failure, taken as a whole, pale in comparison to the most significant source of CRM initiative failure—internal rejection. In this regard, CRM is no different from any other computerization effort. A system can be delivered on-time, to specification, under budget, and work flawlessly from a *technical* basis; however, if a politically powerful group of users rejects the system for whatever reason, then the CRM initiative will fail. At one level, the chances of rejection can be minimized by ensuring that, for each of the major stakeholders (marketing, sales, and customer representatives), the system achieves the following:

- Saves them time
- Makes their job less complex
- Increases their paycheck
- Requires no more effort to use than the system the new initiative is intended to replace

In many cases, the mix is more important than satisfying each parameter. For example, if the CRM system makes a job more complex but increases their paychecks, the added complexity may be acceptable. A common mistake is to assume that because a CRM effort is good for the company, everyone affected by the initiative will automatically rally behind it. Countless IS initiatives have showed this isn't so.

Another avoidable but deadly mistake is to drop a CRM system on a group of users and expect them to use it. Even if the system saves them time, increases their paycheck, and makes at least part of their job less complex, the system may be rejected out of principle. For example, there are numerous cases where the groups that felt excluded from the initial decision-making process eventually killed CRM initiatives that were started without buy-in from every group involved.

In a major Boston teaching hospital, for example, a CRM system was developed to support physician order entry and to provide patients with information on their condition, allow them to schedule appointments, and otherwise address their medical concerns. The system, which took several years and more than $1 million to design and implement, was enthusiastically accepted by patients and their physicians; however, the nursing staff, who were not part of the decision-making process, were infuriated because they were expected to perform most of the data entry, and yet hadn't been consulted in the early phases of the project. Two thousand unionized nurses refused to use the system. The million-dollar system was scratched, and a new system was designed, with a representative from nursing and every other stakeholder in the system.

Returning to the stakeholder analysis, sales, marketing, and customer representatives should have a voice in the CRM approach taken. The group should be charged with helping choose the CRM developer and vendor, as well as the timeline, training requirements and schedule, and other issues related to implementation and use of the system. It's imperative to reach a consensus on these issues before proceeding with implementation.

Making decisions without all of the information is part of being a CEO. Sometimes it's simply unavoidable if the company is to move forward; however, failure to gather some data is inexcusable. For example, before installing a CRM system that will directly affect the sales force, asking salespeople what they need and will use is simply part of due diligence. Problems or predicaments that are external to the company may not be knowable or may cost too much to determine; however, the CEO should know his or her employees and what they will accept and what they won't. As described in the next section, it often isn't so much a matter of whether a particular technology can be of use to various groups within a company as it is a matter of timing.

Time Matters

Time is money, and in the technology space there is the ever-present question of whether to wait or act now. From an economic perspective, the CEO has to determine if his or her company can significantly benefit from a CRM initiative now. The decision depends on a variety of

Customer Value

A basic premise of implementing a CRM solution is that it can improve the bottom line by improving the loyalty of profitable customers; however, the value of a customer is not only increasingly difficult to predict, but unforeseen changes in the market can also drastically shift values. For example, the competition for long-distance customers by MCI, Sprint, and AT&T assumed that once customers switched, they would remain customers for life. As such, companies were willing to pay customers $50 to $100 just for switching over to their service. A similar tactic was instituted by a variety of financial institutions offering charge cards, where one institution would accept a credit card balance transfer from a competing company at a ridiculously low interest rate for a year or more; however, price-sensitive customers—the ones self-selected by the marketing campaigns—learned how to play both the long-distance companies and the charge card companies off each other. Because regular purchases incurred a typical interest rate of up to 20 percent, savvy customers never used the cards for purchases, but simply left the cards at home, exactly what the banks and other financial institutions didn't want.

What's more, these customers didn't develop any degree of loyalty to a particular charge card or long-distance carrier, but switched quickly and easily at the earliest opportunity to save a few cents. As a result, the long-distance telephone business was transformed into an operation with thin margins and virtually no customer loyalty. Similarly, customers may have a half-dozen Visa and MasterCard charge cards from banks they don't even recognize. Lifetime customer value in these industries is virtually zero.

subjective and objective factors, including the CEO's comfort level with risk. A risk-averse CEO may avoid the entire CRM field until one or two clear market leaders appear and the risk of entry is minimal. This approach may mean that the competition benefits from CRM technology now, improving its bottom line and expanding its profitable customer base.

FIGURE 7-5

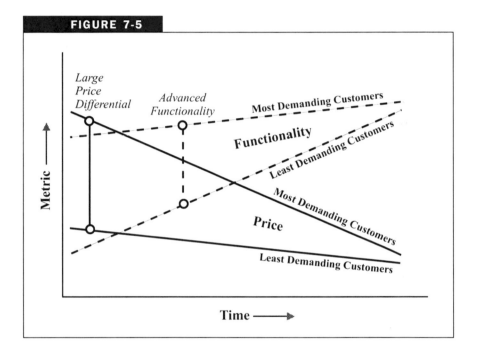

In addition to the subjective issue of timing, there are objective factors to consider as well. As shown in Figure 7-5, most disruptive technologies follow a predictable trajectory. With time, functionality increases while price drops—a pattern seen with PC hardware, for example. Note that customer expectations change with time as well. That is, the most demanding customers require functionality that is greater than that demanded by the least demanding customers, but this difference in expectations diminishes with time. Returning to the PC example, recreational home users often have a computer system with as much RAM, hard disk space, and processor speed as that of high-end business or professional users (i.e., PCs have become commodity items).

Similarly, the price the most demanding users are willing to pay is greater than what the least demanding users are willing to pay, but this difference diminishes with time. Unlike functionality or performance, which increases with time, price tends to drop; however, rise in functionality and drop in price follow different trajectories. As illustrated in Figure 7-5, a technology may be relatively advanced on the functionality curve, whereas the price differential between least to most demanding users may still be great.

The relationship depicted in Figure 7-5 approximates the current state of CRM, in that a wide discrepancy exists in the price of "high-end" and "low-end" solutions; however, the functionality differences between entry-level CRM systems and full-featured ones is less than in earlier offerings. For example, the difference between a fully integrated, stand-alone, $200 contact management system—albeit without advanced data mining and user profiling capabilities—and a full-featured, networked, $10,000 custom application is really a matter of degree, especially when functionality translates into real benefit to the business and the customer. Within the next two or three years, the price differential between the two extremes will drop, with most of the decrease caused by changes in the price the most demanding users are willing to pay.

The question for the CEO is to determine when to make the move to CRM. The early adopter phase, in which the least risk-averse CEOs have started CRM initiatives, is clearly past; however, there are still numerous uncertainties in the space. Assuming the decision is to move ahead, Chapter 8 outlines a process for realizing a CRM initiative with minimum risk and greatest likelihood of success.

> **KEY TERM**
>
> **Early adopter** Someone who embraces a technology before it is generally proven in the marketplace.

Summary

The economics of the CRM space, like the early Web, are relatively volatile. For developers, vendors, and consultants, CRM is the next "new thing," and people and resources are pouring into the space. For the CEO contemplating a CRM initiative, the volatility represents at least a modicum of risk; however, given a knowledge of the investments required, as well as an understanding of major stakeholders involved, it's possible to navigate the CRM space with a smaller degree of economic exposure. Although, with time, the technology and the long-term winners in the CRM arena will become obvious, waiting also has a risk of allowing the competition to realize the benefits of CRM and potentially become more significant competition.

*For the things we have to learn
before we can do them, we learn by
doing them.*

Aristotle

CHAPTER 8

Getting There

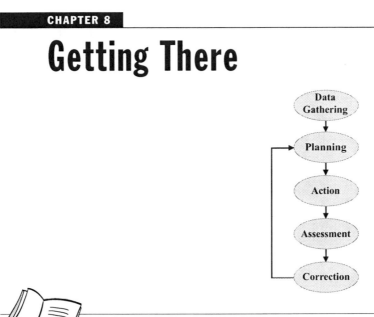

After reading this chapter you will be able to

- Develop a five-phase action plan for implementing CRM in your organization

- Understand how to work with CRM vendors, developers, and consultants

- Recognize and address CRM implementation challenges

- Predict the likely future of CRM

In many respects, this last chapter of *Essentials of CRM,* constitutes the beginning of the journey for the CEO set on realizing the potential of CRM for his or her organization. Whereas the previous chapters laid the technical and economic foundations for understanding the concepts involved in the CRM market or space, this chapter is about exploiting those concepts through taking action. Specifically, this chapter defines a five-phase action plan for implementing or improving CRM in an organization, as outlined in the chapter opening figure.

There are many paths to success and many possible implementation strategies that suit particulars of a given organization; however, the concepts covered here are as applicable to the CEO of a Fortune 500 company as they are to the owner and operator of a small business. With the right approach, customers receive the attention and service they've come to expect, customer service representatives can better serve more customers, and the company can improve its image in the marketplace while improving its bottom line.

Although some companies may use CRM to primarily weed out less profitable customers, the companies that use CRM technologies to cultivate a loyal customer following (e.g., L.L. Bean, Nordstrom, Lands' End, and Amazon.com) create the best of all worlds. These companies place the customer at the center of the retail universe and set the standard for what quality CRM can accomplish. Using an abundance mentality, these companies create a win-win environment in which customers are willing to pay for personal attention. Customers don't go to L.L. Bean or Amazon.com for the best prices. Customers are loyal to these companies because they're made to feel special and valued as a customer.

Before moving to the sections that detail the issues and actions associated with each of the five phases of the action plan, consider the continuation of the roommate story, in the following section, to appreciate a typical CRM installation from the perspective of a CRM consultant.

Life of a Consultant

It has been two years since Debra graduated and moved to the West coast for work. She's still in touch with her old roommates, Paul, who is teaching high school, and Jen, who is married to Bob, and the bike shop owner Hank. Hank is as busy as he wants to be and life is good. He's still happy with the student Debra found to continue the CRM work for him.

TIPS & TECHNIQUES

Hiring a Consultant

The challenge of locating a CRM consultant, like most purchase decisions, includes assessing the quality, cost, and likely ROI. For the highly risk-averse or Fortune 500 company with deep pockets, hiring one of the top-10 consulting firms is a low-risk—albeit expensive—option. For the more financially limited, however, a lower-profile consultancy may be the only option. In this case, the criteria for a consult selection includes:

- *Experience.* How many CRM projects has the consultant or firm been involved with in the past and in what capacity? Success in CRM initiatives is driven as much by experience as it is by innovation.

- *Success rate.* How many CRM projects were successful and how many were unsuccessful? Why?

- *References.* Check them.

- *Rate.* Cost is not necessarily indicative of quality or performance.

- *Insurance.* If the CRM project fails because of consultant error or neglect, does the consultancy have deep enough pockets to cover related losses if found liable in court?

- *Product experience.* Does the consultant have a limited view of CRM products or a more global perspective?

- *Communications skills.* As the intermediary between the CRM vendor, employees, and corporate decision makers, the consultant must have excellent verbal and written communications skills.

- *Background.* Who are the consultant's other customers? Specifically, has the consultancy been employed by the competition? Is there a likelihood of conflict of interest?

For Debra, life has been good as well. After her company went public a year ago, she cashed out her stock options and started a CRM consultancy. Her latest client, a Fortune 500 company, needs her help in the planning phase of a CRM initiative. The company's CIO and IS department have already done some research on the possibilities of CRM, and they want to work with Debra on developing a plan to move forward.

Her first step is to meet with the CEO of the company to get an idea of his expected timeline. Next, Debra asks him to identify the key internal stakeholders who should be involved in the planning meetings. The CEO identifies managers from IS, marketing, sales, the in-house call center, and a representative from the CIO's office to invite to the meetings. The goal of the planning meetings is to define the joint expectations for the CRM system. Debra's role in these meetings is to rein in expectations so that they are in line with the current state of the technology, budget limitations, and what can reasonably be accomplished with a high probability of success.

For example, the sales division of the company would like to have a system that generates leads by identifying customers most likely to be interested in purchasing add-products. The marketing group is interested in segmenting customers by age and income level so they can create custom marketing campaigns targeted at the most lucrative segments of the market. Customer service reps want a solution that will save them the hassle of using two and sometimes three separate programs to answer customer questions. The sales reps want a solution that automatically merges and displays customer purchase history with a contact management system. The CIO is most interested in improving customer loyalty and, by extension, the bottom line. The CEO's goal is to maintain the company's leadership position in the marketplace and fend off major competitors by providing customers with unparalleled support while maintaining the bottom line.

After a month of weekly meetings, Debra presents the group with descriptions of products from four vendors that appear to fit most of the requirements established by the group. One of the products is deficient in marketing and sales support, for example, but provides most of what the customer service representatives want. Similarly, one of the vendors offers a suite of applications that promises everything that everyone wants for each department, but the price tag is out of line with reality.

Over the next month, Debra arranges for presentations from each of the four vendors. During each presentation, Debra asks the vendors to explain how their system is superior to the products from the other three vendors under consideration. She also asks for contact information on satisfied clients who are in the same business as, but who aren't considered competitors with, her client. Over the next three weeks, the group travels to meet six customers who have the systems installed. During the site visits, each of the representatives meets with their respective counterparts to learn everything they can about the positive and negative points of the CRM system installed at their site.

After seeing what solutions are available and workable, Debra and the other members of the implementation committee meet with the CIO to decide whether to move forward, and if so, how. With all of the data at his fingertips, the CEO decides that it's time to move forward. His plan, which is backed by the implementation committee, is to start with a limited implementation that focuses on updating the call center first, and then implementing a data dictionary and data mining applications for sales and marketing. The CEO has the implementation committee submit an RFP and arranges meetings with the top three vendors. After the presentations to the group, and after reviewing the proposal, everyone unanimously selects one of the vendors. After the legal department confirms the contract, the CEO signs on the dotted line.

At this point, Debra's job is nearly finished. She'll drop by to visit the CEO in a few months to help evaluate the implementation. She'll compare it to what the vendor promised to deliver in the contract and to verify that it satisfies most of the expectations of the internal stakeholders. If it doesn't meet expectations, she'll likely be back to help define needed changes in the system. For now, however, she's off to help another customer select a CRM vendor.

This story illustrates not only the life of a typical CRM consultant, but also some of the process involved in implementing a CRM initiative. As illustrated at the beginning of this chapter, the CEO starts out by searching for data on what CRM can do for his company. Based on reading books—like this one—on what CRM is and can do for his company, and working with his CIO and information services staff, he decides to hire a consultant to pull together a plan of action. Based on the recommendations of the implementation committee, the CEO decides to move ahead and signs with a vendor. At this point, it's too early to know if his decisions are correct, but the CEO made every effort to minimize his company's exposure to risk while maximizing the potential to benefit from CRM technology. Now, consider each phase of the implementation plan in detail as follows.

Phase 1: Data Gathering

The first step in the five-phase CRM implementation strategy is data gathering, which, for the most part, constitutes research into exactly what CRM has to offer the company. Data gathering can involve reading, attending seminars, talking to colleagues, assigning someone inside the organization to research the subject and report back to the CEO, or, as in the story, hiring a consultant.

From this research, the CEO should have an idea of the technologies available for CRM, a realistic timeline for implementation, an idea of the costs involved, and examples of companies that benefited from investing in CRM. The CEO should also have an understanding of his or her company, including who within the company has a stake in— and should have a say in—deciding on the details of the implementation approach.

It's a mistake to believe that a simple dictate from the CEO will convince everyone to fall in line with a CRM project. In reality, the politics of corporate America require a buy-in at every level in the organization. This means establishing a small implementation committee with representatives from each of the major stakeholders; typically, a representative is chosen from sales, marketing, customer support, and the CIO's office. One or two customers of the appropriate demographic might be included in the committee as well in order to provide a window into the user's perspective on the CRM effort.

Metrics for Success

Metrics for success, such as improvements in the bottom line and behavior changes in customers and employees, are defined in the data gathering phase. Desirable behavior changes typically include fewer customer interactions with customer service representatives and more customer interaction with the corporate Web site; greater use of E-mail in contact customer support; more self-entry of customer data into the corporate database; and more repeat business from the most profitable customers. Some of the possible employee behavior changes include an increase in the number of calls per hour handled by customer service reps; more effective use of the company's database by marketing and sales representatives; fewer internal calls to technical support; and more effective use of corporate information resources in general.

Metrics for success should be defined in absolute, quantitative terms. For example, a payback period of two years with a 5 percent savings for three years after that is an example of an absolute metric. The hazard in projecting past five years with a technology-based initiative of any type is the great likelihood that a disruptive technology will be introduced that "changes everything." For example, although eCRM is an active area, within five years the Web may be fully transformed from what it is today into an unrecognizable system. If all goes according to some predictions, the Internet may be most useful as an alternative to the telephone, which will certainly change how eCRM is provided.

It's important to be specific about what success means in the data gathering phase of the process. When everyone involved starts working on the actual implementation of the project it's easy to forget about the overall purpose of the project, and to instead focus on succeeding in each phase along the way. Although this myopia may be necessary at the lower levels in the organization, the CEO needs to keep the larger picture in plain view at all times.

Phase 2: Planning

As in the story, the planning phase is the first real step taken within the organization to move the CRM initiative from theory to practice. The fundamental decisions to be made during the planning phase pertain to what has to be done and who will do it. To define this, requirements specification and functional specification documents are prepared. They include cost estimates, resource requirements, and an explicit estimate of ROI. They also establish a timeline that identifies the major milestones along the way toward a CRM solution. The time and consideration invested in the planning phase can pay large dividends later, during actual implementation.

Timeline

One of the major aspects of planning a CRM implementation is defining a workable timeline. Although the absolute times allotted each task

---

FIGURE 8-1

CRM Implementation Milestones

Identify critical success factors.
Establish implementation committee.
Identify project scope, goals, and objectives.
Determine resource requirements.
Define requirements specifications.
      Rank-order importance of features.
      Determine feasibility.
Define project management.
      Identify internal expert or consultant.
Evaluate product.
      Establish cost estimates.
Review functional specifications.
      Review hardware requirements.
      Review communications standards.
      Review ancillary application requirements.
Select vendor.
      Announce RFP.
      Visit sites.
      Attend vendor presentations.
Sign contract.
Start development.
Install system.
Integrate with existing systems and infrastructure users.
Roll out.
Sign off.
Maintain system.

---

and milestone will vary according to the resources available, the complexity of the installation, and the expertise of the people involved, the key implementation milestones generally include those listed in Figure 8-1.

Note that various types of expertise are required at different points in the timeline. For example, the consultant or internal resource used to help define the expectations and requirements of the CRM system may be different from the person assigned the responsibility of project management. Similarly, the implementation committee may need to look to various sources of expertise in evaluating products and vendors.

Resource Requirements

The resources required for a CRM implementation are a function of the corporation's expectations, whether a full or limited implementation is planned, and the vendor's timeline. Other internal projects may demand resources that delay the projected implementation timeline. Some resources must be in place before others. For example, before a data mining application can be installed, a prerequisite is a functional data warehouse or an equivalent data store that can be searched. Similarly, the requirements of the new CRM software may dictate an operating system upgrade, which may take months in an organization with hundreds of PCs and several servers. In addition, upgrading the operating system may require other programs to be upgraded as well. Upgrading several applications and the operating system on hundreds of PCs in a call center without causing disruption in service can take months. Other prerequisite resource requirements may include sales, marketing, and call center representative training. If the new system is likely to have a major impact on customers, then a marketing campaign to set customer expectations may have to be defined and coordinated with the release timeline.

In addition to evaluating the resource requirements for implementation, the total cost of ownership (TCO) over the life of the system should be considered. There are likely to be significant recurring costs, in addition to the upfront costs, such as monthly Internet connection charges, insurance, and maintaining an inventory of spare PCs, headsets, and related hardware. Additional factors to consider include the mean time before replacement (MTBR) for software and hardware, power requirements, theft potential, portability, and fragility. These factors are especially relevant when the CRM solution is delivered on a portable device, such as a salesperson's laptop.

KEY TERMS

Total cost of ownership (TCO) The cost of owning a device or technology, including operating expenses. For example, the total cost of owning a PC includes training, software, power, Internet connection charges, lost productivity caused by inexperience with a PC instead of working on the project at hand, and lost opportunity costs. Similarly, the cost of owning a piece of software includes not only the purchase cost, but maintenance costs as well.

Mean time before replacement (MTBR) The average time interval, usually expressed in hours, that will elapse before a system is no longer optimal and is replaced by a better (i.e., faster, smaller, less expensive, or cheaper to operate) system.

Solving potential resource requirement problems can require compromise. For example, delivering CRM to a mobile sales force on portable hardware platforms, such as wireless, handheld personal digital assistants (PDAs), increases theft potential. Less expensive, larger, heavier portable units may be less attractive to a thief, but the sales force may shy away from the units as well.

Project Management

The resource requirements defined in the planning stage include people and technology. From a human resource perspective, at least one full-time equivalent—either a CRM technology specialist who is hired from a consultancy or an internal specialist—should be assigned to the implementation project. The person's skill set should include project management, working with vendors, knowledge of the industry, knowledge of CRM, references, and experience with E-commerce and the Web in general.

A key issue in the management of CRM implementation is whether to use in-house expertise or look to an external consultancy. The advantages and disadvantages of using internal expertise for project management are summarized in Figure 8-2.

FIGURE 8-2

Advantages of Using Internal Expertise

Decreased motivation for secondary gain
Increased control
Increased security
Increased sensitivity to the corporate culture
Increased time savings
Minimal filtering of information
Political advantage

Disadvantages of Using Internal Expertise

Increased potential for distraction
Isolation
Lack of experience
Less vendor involvement

One of the advantages of relying on an internal resource is increased control. An employee can be redirected as necessary, without an added layer of management or having to deal with the politics of an external consultancy. The loyalty of an internal resource is also clear; he or she is primarily accountable to the company, not an outside vendor or agency. In addition, because the reporting structure is internal and not colored to hide the mistakes or miscalculations of a vendor or external consultancy, there is usually less filtering of information that may be critical for the company to know. Unless the employee is looking for a career move, he or she is less susceptible to manipulation by developers and vendors than are consultants.

Regardless of whether mutual nondisclosure agreements are in place, the use of an outside consultant represents an increased security risk. Even if unintentional, trade secrets, including internal processes, are less likely to fall into the hands of a competitor when a consultant is involved. An employee simply has less opportunity to interact with the competition.

Using an internal resource can save time. An employee is, by definition, already on the payroll and available for work. A consultant, in contrast, has to learn the environment, who the players are, and what can't be said. That is, an employee is more sensitive to the corporate culture. An employee is more likely to be able to maneuver around internal challenges that a consultant would not fully grasp. In addition, an internal resource may have the political influence necessary to get the CRM system accepted where a consultant would not. Someone recruited from within the company doesn't have to invest the time and energy to learn who the major stakeholders are in the company.

Although the advantages of using an internal resource may be significant, using an internal resource to manage a major CRM project may also be problematic. A disadvantage of using someone already on the payroll to manage a CRM implementation is the increased potential for distraction. An employee, unlike an outside consultant assigned to a single task, may be pulled away from the CRM effort to put out other fires. Although the flexibility to have staff available to put out fires can be useful, it's a negative factor from the perspective of completing a CRM implementation.

Lack of experience in the CRM space is also a potential pitfall associated with using inside expertise. Unless he or she is a recent hire, an employee likely lacks hands-on experience in leading-edge CRM. In some ways, isolation is part of many corporate cultures. Although it may make for a more consistent workforce, an employee steeped in corporate culture isn't likely to learn about the mistakes of others in the industry as quickly as a consultant would.

Finally, relying on an internal resource can often decrease the efficiency with which vendors can work with the company. Troubleshooting a suite of programs pulled together by an internal resource can be difficult because of lack of rapport with vendors. Without direct support, such as what a consultant associated with a vendor might offer, cases of fingerpointing are common. In other words, because there is no direct tie to the vendor or at least no record of accomplishment of working together on a project, the internal manager may be faulted for any problems that arise. When faced with a problem report, the vendor may ignore an employee's input in identifying the source of problems.

It's simply easier for a vendor to accuse a company representative or blame a company process they don't know very well. There is also the increased likelihood of fingerpointing, simply because the vendor is unfamiliar with the internal resource. Consider the typical situation in which a CRM application fails to work to specifications, for example, performance is unsatisfactory, as measured in the number of transactions that can be processed per minute. The possible variables include incorrectly configured hardware, the incorrect operating system version or incorrect settings, an incorrectly installed application, or problems with the networking infrastructure. In all cases, the common factor is human —consultant—error. Without confidence in the consultant, a vendor's supposition is typically that the consultant made an error somewhere along the way in installing and configuring their product.

It's possible to outsource all or part of a CRM implementation. As shown in Figure 8-3, the entire call center can be outsourced as a component of an eCRM suite, to the point that the call center and eCRM software can be located remotely. In fact, the ASP Web server can be located somewhere in the states and the call center proper can be located in India, where customer service representatives use the eCRM software to help domestic callers. In addition, with ASP technology and modern telephone switching, it's possible for customer service reps to answer customer calls from home even when the company's main phone number is dialed—a practice pioneered by the 900 services.

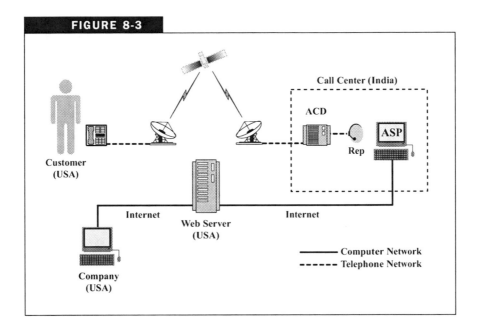

Full-Scale versus Limited Implementation

A major milestone in CRM implementation is determining the scope of the project. One extreme is to implement a proof of concept, focusing on a single department or a subset of a department, such as the mobile division of a national or regional sales force. The other extreme is to implement a full CRM solution for every employee in sales, marketing, and customer support. Whether to go for a full-scale implementation, a limited CRM implementation, or somewhere in between depends on the budget, time constraints, corporate politics, legal issues, the status and direction of the competition, the experience of the available resources, and the advice from consultants.

FIGURE 8-4

Advantages

Competitive advantage
Cost savings
Significant ROI
Vendor attentiveness

Disadvantages

Decreased technologic flexibility
Difficult buy-in
Greater dependency
Greater disruption
Increased risk exposure
Increased stress
Increased susceptibility
Large capital commitment
More time required

The potential advantages and disadvantages of a full-scale or nearly full-scale CRM implementation are listed in Figure 8-4. The most obvious factor to consider in making this determination is finances. A large capital commitment may simply not be possible, even though some vendors claim that the full ROI of a CRM initiative can only be realized with a full implementation, and that the ROI of anything less can't be realistically evaluated. In addition, implementing a total CRM solution may be less expensive than buying and installing components piecemeal or in limited quantities. One workaround is to mitigate the immediate impact of a large capital outlay by working with a vendor to develop an extended payment schedule.

An advantage of a full-scale CRM implementation is that it may provide a company significant advantage over the competition if it is successful. In this regard, a full-scale implementation generally increases the attention a vendor pays to the project. Because more is at risk, vendors tend to invest proportionately more in larger projects, thereby increasing the odds of success.

A full-scale CRM implementation is usually less challenging and costly for all involved if there is no legacy CRM system to deal with. There are no interfaces to write in order to share data with older systems and no hardware or software limitations, such as outdated operating systems, to deal with; however, with the exception of new call centers, few installations are totally void of equipment and software that may need to be upgraded or disposed of.

Another potentially significant disadvantage of a full-scale CRM implementation is an overall decrease in technologic flexibility. Committing to a full-scale initiative that embraces one technology over another makes the company more susceptible to having its systems rendered obsolete by a disruptive technology. For example, if Microsoft's XP operating system, together with its .NET telephony initiative, is successful, it will change the way telephones are used in CRM; telephones will disappear as devices separate from a networked PC. As such, a company's investment in software and hardware dedicated to traditional systems may not provide the expected ROI, in part because it will have to be replaced earlier than expected. With a limited implementation, it's much easier to write the system off as a learning experience.

A full-scale implementation generally takes more time, during which more can happen that isn't directly related to the project. For example, compared to a quick, limited implementation, a full-scale implementation that unfolds over many months (or years) is more susceptible to external problems, such as worker shortages and economic downturns. With an economic downturn, for example, layoffs combined with anxiety about job loss can decrease employee effectiveness and morale.

In a larger company, some internal group will probably resist some part of a full-scale, corporatewide implementation. Universal buy-in is more difficult in part because of the increased risk exposure associated with a full-scale implementation. The entire company or an entire department may be reliant on a single developer and vendor. If the vendor fails, for example, it's not likely that another company will be able to take over the project and maintain the initial timeline, simply because of the complexity of a full-scale implementation.

There is also the factor of increased disruption. The business will be disrupted to some degree even if the project is completely successful. Complete disruption of the business process is possible if the CRM

FIGURE 8-5

Advantages—Competency Assessment

Less exposure to risk
Lower resource requirements
Political test bed
Proof of concept
Quick win
Shorter timeline

Disadvantages—Competitive Disadvantage

Infrastructure costs
Limited ROI
More total time
No critical mass
Scaling not guaranteed

implementation fails. Hardware and software aside, there is greater risk of employee burnout because of the increased stress associated with bringing a full-scale CRM package online.

The potential advantages and disadvantages of a limited CRM implementation are shown in Figure 8-5. The most obvious advantages are lower resource requirements, including a lower initial cash outlay and lower exposure to risk. A limited implementation is usually the best route for a quick win, in that a limited engagement with "low-lying fruit"—a quick, easy win—in one department can encourage other departments to get behind a full-scale effort. A proof of concept, developed and deployed in a short time, is also a way to assess the competency of vendors and consultants before embarking on a more extensive and expensive endeavor. The proof of concept allows internal process/political issues that may not be obvious to be identified without a test to stir up potential internal adversaries.

The potential disadvantages of embarking on a limited CRM implementation are linked to economic and technologic risks. For example, the company may not realize a significant ROI, even though infrastructure costs may be the same as for a full system. In addition, the system may not scale as expected, given that a successful limited implementation does not guarantee a successful full-scale implementation. From a human resource perspective, there may not be a critical mass of applications needed to encourage or entice employees in the affected departments to learn and use the new CRM system.

A company taking a limited approach may be at a competitive disadvantage if competitors successfully manage a full-scale implementation. In addition, when it comes to catching up to the competition, building a system piecemeal may extend the time for a full-scale implementation.

Phase 3: Action

In simplest terms, the action phase of a CRM implementation involves making the plan developed in Phase 2 a reality. Following the timeline established during the planning stage, the implementation committee performs due diligence by evaluating the products available and compiling cost estimates. Site visits, interviews, and other sources of data are evaluated as necessary. Technical details, such as hardware requirements, the standards used in the system, and add-on or ancillary software requirements are reviewed in depth, often with the help of a CRM consultant.

With the top two or three products that best fit the constraints imposed by the implementation committee identified, the committee announces a request for proposal (RFP) and reviews the responses. A contract is negotiated, signed, and development is begun. A kickoff meeting is typically established at this point, in part to enjoin the key players in the organization, including the representatives on the implementation committee. During the kickoff meeting, the vendor may help articulate the vision, perhaps by bringing in someone that the group respects from another site that had success with the product.

After the system is developed, integrated with existing systems if necessary, and tested, the appropriate users are trained in preparation for deployment. The selection of beta testers is important because they will probably be instrumental, even if only in an unofficial capacity, in introducing the system to others in the enterprise. A marketing campaign, either internally or externally focused, is begun around this time as well. If there are no bug fixes or process oversights, the system is deployed to the degree defined in the implementation plan, starting with the official rollout event. Because of the hype surrounding CRM technology, the rollout must be accompanied by a carefully orchestrated plan of employee expectation management.

With the proper support, training, political positioning, and ongoing maintenance, the system should be used as it was designed. Regardless of how well the development effort turned out, the degree to which the implementation fulfills the company's needs as a CRM tool must be assessed, as described as follows.

Phase 4: Assessment

The CRM system should be assessed at predefined intervals, (e.g., quarterly) for overall impact on the company. Evaluation should include the metrics defined in the data gathering phase, such as change in the number of calls handled by customer support per hour, Web site activity, the number of new sales, and the quantity and quality of new data that can be used by sales and marketing. The degree to which the system fulfills the requirements and functional specifications and the vendor's claims can also establish an assessment guideline. Customer and user experience, based on user and customer polls, make other useful metrics.

If the goal is to give customers a positive experience, then poll customers and ask if they like the service. If a goal is to dissuade certain groups of customers from calling customer support, then measure the number of calls from nonprofitable customers. Determine if there is a drop in the number of calls, a change in the average time on hold, or a change in the bottom line. Although the time reps spend with unprofitable customers may be down, it may take some time for them to leave the system.

In assessing the implementation, a limiting factor is the lag time between rollout and measurable impact. By the time the results are in, a CRM system may prove to be a disaster; hence the advantage of a limited implementation. The extent of assessment depends on which components of a CRM package have been implemented. Even if a comprehensive system is in place, it usually makes sense to focus the assessment on one component at a time.

Phase 5: Correction

The five-phase action plan is a positive feedback loop, in that the results of the assessment phase can and should be used to improve the system. One way to carry this plan out is to compile the information on what failed and where corrections are necessary and present it to the original implementation committee.

It will probably be necessary to add members to the original committee because of inevitable problems that will be uncovered that may not have been obvious during the initial planning. For example, if the customer service representative response time increased significantly with the introduction of the system, which of the following are introducing the delay:

- Is it process, hardware, or software?
- Is the slowdown caused by a lack of training?
- Are there software bugs?
- Is it the computer hardware performance?
- Is the telecom equipment at fault?
- Are customer service reps intentionally slowing down the system?
- Is the interface between the telephone and computer network functioning properly?

Because there are typically more questions than answers at this phase of the project, employees with expertise in various areas of the company, from HR to IS, may need to be called on for advice.

Given the findings, a relevant question to ask at this phase of the action plan is whether the error is significant enough to warrant a change or whether a workaround process could be instituted later. In this regard, the five-phase process is begun anew, using data gathered during the assessment phase.

As a result of the correction phase, the timeline, technologies, metrics, requirements, and functional specifications are updated, with a goal of creating an iterative, stepwise improvement that is in line with the company's overall CRM goals.

Implementation Challenges

Each phase of the action plan is associated with challenges that must be adequately addressed in order for the plan to move forward. Borrowing concepts from chemical processes, implementation challenges can be viewed as the *energy of activation* that must be overcome in order for the action plan to move forward (see Figure 8-6).

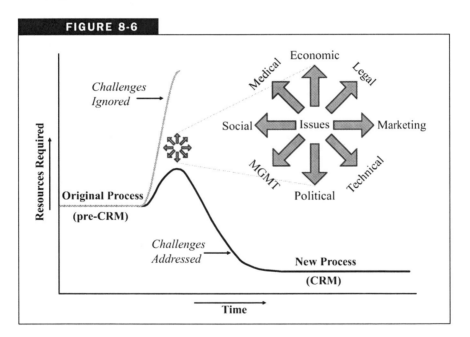

FIGURE 8-6

As illustrated in Figure 8-6, the key implementation challenges fall into eight categories:

1. Management

2. Political

3. Economic

4. Medical

5. Legal

6. Technical

7. Marketing

8. Social

Implementing a CRM initiative should result in a new process that eventually requires less in the way of resources, including time and money. Implementing the action plan requires resources; however, if the implementation challenges are properly addressed, the increase in resource requirements is relatively small and manageable (solid line). Ignoring the challenges may result in extremely high resource requirements, however, and the project will likely stall.

The more significant challenges within each of the eight areas, listed in Figure 8-7, may or may not be relevant to a particular implementation, depending on the company, the extent of the implementation, the technologies involved, and the goals of CRM implementation. The idea is to recognize the potential for these and other challenges to arise and to proactively address them before they can cause a problem.

For example, increasing the throughput of each call center rep, which may require more keyboard or mouse activity, may result in increased repetitive strain injury (RSI) claims, valid or otherwise. The potential legal and medical challenges can be addressed by purchasing ergonomic keyboards, such as the Microsoft Natural Keyboard, supplying wrist rests for mice, and training reps on how to adjust their chair height relative to their keyboard to minimize the risk of injury. Ensuring proper lighting, encouraging personalization of cubicle space, providing outlets for stress, and paying attention to other "creature comforts" can help circumvent employee burnout and other symptoms characteristic of high-pressure, isolated cubicle life.

FIGURE 8-7

Management	Legal
Developer evaluation	Customer privacy
Diversion of resources	Fraud
Implementation strategy	Intellectual property
Initial focus	RSI claims
Technologic details	**Technical**
Vendor evaluation	Archiving
Volatility of the CRM space	Complexity
Political	Hardware platform
Local government	Infrastructure capacity
OSHA regulations	Interfaces
Standards organizations	Localization
Telecom legislation	Responsiveness
Economic	Scalability
Competition	Security
Critical mass of applications	Standards
Economic environment	Usability
Infrastructure investment	**Marketing**
Lost opportunity costs	Business myopia
Relevance of E-commerce	Heightened expectations
Speculation	Product divergence
Strategic partnerships	**Social**
Time pressure	Demand for quality support
Medical	Privacy
Burn-out	Timing
Cubicle environment	

Even reps who use other interfaces, such as voice recognition, are potential legal liabilities. For example, several claims have been made against employers by reps who use voice recognition software and develop voice problems, such as polyps (small nodules) on their vocal cords—conditions commonly found in singers and drill sergeants. Successful legal claims can be avoided by providing proper training, ensuring that reps are allowed periodic breaks, and emphasizing that reps use common sense when using equipment.

Some of the more significant political challenges are related to compliance with Occupational Safety and Health Administration (OSHA) regulations, as well as local government regulations regarding employees and work environments. There are also the challenges of complying with standards of organizations that allow call center interoperability, sales force automation with wireless and portable devices, and other communications standards. For example, there may be competition for spectrum space for wireless PDAs and laptops with other wireless services, such as local fire and police. State and federal telecom legislation can affect the rates of leased telephone lines, the availability and cost of operating a PBX, and other commercial telephone equipment. In this regard, larger companies may want to be involved in lobbying efforts aimed at controlling the increase of local and long-distance commercial telephone rates.

From an economic perspective, the CRM space is filled with challenges. For one, the CRM space, like the early Web space, is largely speculative. Investing in a high-speed, fiberoptic infrastructure for a call center, for example, may pay out in the end because of increased throughput; however, the infrastructure may prove to be a poor investment if advances in high-speed wireless connectivity become commercially viable.

Technically, literally hundreds of potential problems are associated with a CRM implementation. As noted earlier, one issue is scalability. A system that is installed on 10 PCs that works as expected may not work when the system is expanded to 100 PCs because of limitations in the software, supporting infrastructure, hardware, or the process involved in directing calls to the proper customer service representative. Similarly, a trial of a dozen handheld mobile PDAs used by the sales force may not scale to a 1000-rep sales force because of regional limitations in connecting to the wireless Web and Internet. These sorts of surprises can be proactively addressed by more thorough developer and vendor evaluations. Management may decide, for example, to try a trial of two competing wireless technologies to support sales representatives, instead of evaluating only one potential solution.

As noted throughout this book, one of the marketing challenges is dealing with heightened customer expectations. Given the hype associated with the wireless Web and components of pervasive computing, many customers increasingly expect that customer service, like other products and services that can be had at the click of a button, can be delivered on demand. The divergence of CRM products that are variably used to respond immediately to profitable customers and with significant delays to others can cause confusion in the CRM space.

From a social perspective, the chief challenge is overcoming customer concerns regarding the privacy of their communications and transactions. Customers generally expect that the details of their online purchases will not be sold to other companies and that their personal charge card numbers and other information will be safe.

The management challenges are generally related to controlling risk. For example, there are technologic risks such as obsolescence with the emergence of new technologies. The risk can be minimized through the judicious selection of partnerships with vendors, focusing initially on areas in the company most likely to respond to a CRM effort and carefully formulating an implementation strategy.

Future of CRM

Intelligent refrigerators that notify customers that it's time to buy more milk and cars that automatically notify the driver when the manufacturer issues a recall are all part of an inevitable future. The questions are how and when, not if, the customer-centric view of commerce that is

IN THE REAL WORLD

Legal Matters

Contrary to vendor advertisements, not every CRM initiative ends with a satisfied customer, and lawsuits are increasingly common. For example, CarsDirect.com sued its CRM consultant for recommending a CRM solution that CarsDirect claims ultimately cost the company tens of millions of dollars in lost business and productivity. Of note is that the CRM software vendor was not named in the suit, as per terms of the product license. Virtually all software licenses, from PC to mainframe applications, widely disclaim any warranty regarding the performance or suitability of the software for any particular purpose.

being codified in evolving CRM technologies will be the norm. In this regard, timing is everything, and the longevity of current offerings in the CRM space should be viewed with guarded optimism.

The potential benefits of CRM are obvious, and yet many of the obvious applications of computerization have yet to be embraced by users. For example, although electronic medical record systems have been available for decades, only 2 or 3 percent of hospitals use this technology. Despite the ready availability of software and hardware that complements the practice of medicine, most patient records are maintained on paper. Most electronic medical record systems are inefficient, don't save the nurses and physicians time, are only minimally accessible by patients, and in general complicate the practice of medicine.

In the short term, the risks of failure are real; however, the risk can be managed or at least minimized by learning from the successes and mistakes of others who have implemented CRM in a variety of industries. For example, most failures in the CRM space are caused by errors and oversights in planning, in failing to take users into account, in not enjoining the stakeholders and users behind a CRM effort, and of set-ting unrealistic goals, not technologic limitations.

In this regard, although the CIO and computer professionals may work out the technical aspects of a CRM effort, only the CEO is in a position to broker a CRM initiative to all the major players in an organization. That is, success in the CRM space isn't so much a function of technology as it is a clear vision of the future of the corporation, an understanding of the needs of the key stakeholders, a clear definition of the expected outcome of the CRM initiative, and leadership. Success in this and any other cor-poratewide project depends on the leadership capabilities of the CEO, especially the ability to create an infectious feeling of positive optimism.

Summary

In the current economic environment, where attracting and keeping profitable customers can mean the difference between commercial success or failure, CRM technology can help. Properly implemented, CRM technology and associated behavior changes become the means by which customers of large companies can access information and other assistance in a timely, friendly, respectful manner that approximates what customers have come to expect from the shopkeeper at the corner store.

CRM, like the Web and other technologies and business processes, is evolving. As such, entering the CRM fray has a risk and a cost; how-ever, not only does ignoring CRM have a cost as well, but unlike taking action, there is no ROI associated with inactivity.

Implementing a CRM initiative requires a plan of action that not only details the processes and milestones involved but also includes pro-visions for inevitable challenges that will appear along the way. The five-phase action plan offered here, like any other implementation plan, has to be modified to suit the needs of a particular project and the vision and personality of the CEO.

Seasoned CEOs know that risk of failure and the prospect for gain are inexorably linked. They know that acting with low expectations usually results in little or no disappointments, but also produces mediocre results. Similarly, they know that the downside of working toward a goal with only modest expectations is only modest disappointment; however, truly great leaders set great expectations for themselves, the company, and their customers. The downside—a risk great leaders are willing to take—is great disappointment; however, visionary CEOs, appropriately grounded in the facts of the CRM space, are focused on the upside—exceptional achievement and extraordinary customer service.

Destiny is not a matter of chance; it is a matter of choice. It is not something to be waited for; but, rather something to be achieved.

William Jennings Bryan

Further Reading

Books

Anderson, K., and R. Zemke (1998). *Delivering Knock Your Socks Off Service.* New York: AMACOM.

Bailey, K. and K. Leland (2001). *Online Customer Service for Dummies.* New York: Hungry Minds, Inc.

Bergeron, B. (2001). *The Eternal E-Customer: How Emotionally Intelligent Interfaces Can Create Long-Lasting Customer Relationships.* New York: McGraw-Hill.

Blanchard, K., and S. Bowles (1993). *Raving Fans: A Revolutionary Approach to Customer Service.* New York: William Morrow and Company, Inc.

Cohan, P. (2000). *e-Profit.* New York: American Management Association.

Davis, S. (2000). *Brand Asset Management.* San Francisco: Jossey-Bass, Inc.

Eichenwald, K. (2000). *The Informant.* New York, Broadway Books.

Garfield, S. (2000). *Database Nation: The Death of Privacy in the 21st Century.* Sebastopl, CA: O'Riley & Associates, Inc.

Gilmonre, J., and B. Pine, eds. (2000). *Markets of One: Creating Customer-Unique Value Through Mass Customization.* Boston: Harvard Business Review.

Greenberg, P. (2001). *CRM at the Speed of Light.* New York: McGraw-Hill.

Gschwandtner, G. (1996). *Selling Power's Best.* Fredericksburg, VA: Personal Selling Power, Inc.

Hall, E. (1998). *Managing Risk: Methods for Software Systems Development.* Reading, MA: Addison-Wesley.

Hartman, A., J. Sifonis, and J Kador. (1999). *Net Ready: Strategies for Success in the E-Conomy.* New York: McGraw-Hill.

Horibe, F. (1999). *Managing Knowledge Workers*. Etobicoke, Ontario: John Wiley & Sons Canada Limited.

Humphries, M., M. Day, and M. Hawkins. (1999). *Data Warehousing Architecture and Implementation*. Upper Saddle River, NJ: Prentice Hall.

Johnson, S. (2000). *Who Moved My Cheese?* Newark, NJ: Penguin Putnam, Inc.

Johnson, S. (1997). *Interface Culture: How New Technology Transforms the Way We Create and Communicate*. San Francisco: HarperEdge.

Keen, P., C. Ballance, S. Chan, and S. Schrump. *Electronic Commerce Relationships: Trust by Design*. Upper Saddle River, NJ: Prentice Hall PTR.

Kessler, S. (1996). *Measuring and Managing Customer Satisfaction: Going for the Gold*. Milwaukee: ASQC Quality Press.

Lee, D. (2000). *The Customer Relationship Management Survival Guide*. St. Paul: HYM Press.

Mackay, H. (1988). *Swim with the Sharks Without Being Eaten Alive*. New York: Ballantine Books.

McKean, J. (1999). *Information Masters*. New York: John Wiley & Sons, Inc.

McKenzie, R. (2001). *The Relationship-Based Enterprise*. New York: McGraw-Hill.

Murphy, T. (2000). *Web Rules: How the Internet is Changing the Way Consumers Make Choices*. Chicago: Dearborn Financial Publishing.

Nelson, B. (1994). *1001 Ways to Reward Employees*. New York, Workman Publishing.

Newell, F. (2000). *Loyalty.com*. New York: McGraw-Hill.

Nykamp, M. (2001). The Customer Differential. New York: AMACOM.

Oppliger, R. (1998). *Internet and Intranet Security*. Norwood, MA: Artech House, Inc.

Rodin, R. (1999). *Free, Perfect, and Now*. New York: Simon & Schuster, Inc.

Seybold, P. (2001). *The Customer Revolution*. New York: Crown Business.

Seybold, P. (1998). *Customer.com*. New York: Time Books.

Simon, A. (1997). *Data Warehousing for Dummies*. Foster City, CA: IDG Books Worldwide, Inc.

Smith, E. (2000). *e-Loyalty: How to Keep Customers Coming Back to Your Website*. New York: HarperBusiness.

Smith, R., M. Speaker, and M. Thompson. (2000). *The Complete Idiot's Guide to e-Commerce*. Indianapolis: QUE.

Swift, R. (2001). *Accelerating Customer Relationships: Using CRM and Relationship Technologies*. Upper Saddle River, NJ: Prentice Hall PTR.

Sykes, C. (1999). *The End of Privacy*. New York: St. Martins Press.

Wellington, P. (1995). *Kaizen Strategies for Customer Care*. New York: Prentice Hall.

Monthly Publications

CRM Magazine. www.CRMmag.com—the magazine for CRM.

SC Magazine. www.SCMagazine.com—covers security issues, including reviews of latest software and federal legislation.

Glossary

Bot   A software robot that can be programmed to perform a variety of tasks, from locating a Web page containing a particular word or phrase, to replying to text statements and questions in real time.

Communications protocol A set of standards designed to allow computers to exchange data.

Cookie. A file written to a customer's hard drive by a Web server that identifies the customer on subsequent visits to the site.

Customer relationship management (CRM) The dynamic process of managing a customer-company relationship such that customers elect to continue mutually beneficial commercial exchanges and are dissuaded from participating in exchanges that are unprofitable to the company.

Developer The creator of a software product (e.g., Microsoft and Oracle).

Disruptive technology A technology that empowers a different group of users and gets better over time. The PC is a disruptive technology, in that it empowered individuals to perform tasks once relegated to large data centers.

Early adopter Someone who embraces a technology before it is generally proven in the marketplace.

E-commerce The sale of goods and services over the Web.

Encryption The process of encoding data to prevent someone without the proper key from understanding the data, even though they may have access to the data. Because all encryption schemes can be broken with time, user authentication is considered more secure.

Enterprise resource planning (ERP) The category of software designed to improve the internal processes of a company.

Ergonomics The system describing the physical relationship between the user and the computer and telecommunications hardware. The shape and layout of the keyboard, fit and weight of the telephone headset, room lighting, chair height and contour, desk and monitor height, monitor quality, and ambient lighting are all ergonomic factors that can enhance or decrease the effectiveness of a customer service representative.

Ethernet A high-speed network standard that is often used to connect PCs, servers, printers, modems, and other peripherals.

Functional specifications The technical document that specifies exactly what a software and/or hardware system will deliver, in terms of response time, bandwidth, what data elements will be stored, exactly what each report contains, and other quantitative measures. A typical statement in a functional specification document would read "customer service representatives will be presented with the customer's prior purchases within 3 seconds of depressing the <F3> key."

Marketing The process associated with promoting products or services for sale, traditionally involving product, price, place, and promotion.

Mean time before replacement (MTBR) The average time interval, usually expressed in hours, that will elapse before a system is no longer optimal and is replaced by a better (i.e., faster, smaller, less expensive, or cheaper to operate) system.

Repetitive strain injury (RSI) A disorder of the tendons, ligaments, and nerves caused by repeated, prolonged repetitious movements, such as typing on a keyboard. The most common form of RSI in customer service representatives is carpal tunnel syndrome, which affects the wrists and hands, and can result in the temporary total loss of functionality of the hands.

Requirements specifications The qualitative document that specifies the needs that must be addressed by a particular technology. The requirements specification is written in language such as "the CRM system will allow marketing to sort customers by age."

Sales The process of selling, or exchanging money for products and services.

Sales force automation (SFA) The software category designed to facilitate the sales process. Contact management packages are often classified as sales force automation tools.

Telematics Mobile computing and telecommunications.

Telephony The transmission and reception of voice and data.

Text-to-speech (TTS) A technology based on the generation of spoken English (or other language), based on text input. The problem with most TTS systems or engines is that the sounds are somewhat mechanical and do not convey the subtle inflections of human speech, although today's computer voices are intelligible.

Total cost of ownership (TCO) The cost of owning a device or technology, including operating expenses. For example, the total cost of owning a PC includes training, software, power, Internet connection charges, lost productivity due to inexperience with a PC instead of working on the project at hand, and lost opportunity costs. Similarly, the cost of owning a piece of software includes not only the purchase cost, but maintenance costs as well.

Vendor The seller of software products. Vendors are typically value-added resellers of products that may be bundled with other products and services, such as training. In some cases, the vendor and developer are one company.

Voice recognition The ability of a computer to recognize the spoken word for the purpose of data input and receiving commands. Also called speech recognition.

Index